Dangerous Guesswork In Economic Policy

Max Steuer

Dangerous Guesswork In Economic Policy

Illustrations by Jon Riley

 Springer

Max Steuer
Department of Economics
London School of Economics
London, UK

ISBN 978-3-031-56077-4   ISBN 978-3-031-56078-1   (eBook)
https://doi.org/10.1007/978-3-031-56078-1

This Springer imprint is published by the registered company Springer Nature Switzerland AG
The registered company address is: Gewerbestrasse 11, 6330 Cham, Switzerland

If disposing of this product, please recycle the paper.

By the Same Author

Non-Fiction

Books

Mathematical Sociology (with Janet Holland) (Weidenfeld & Nicolson, 1969)
The Impact of Foreign Direct Investment on the United Kingdom (HMSO,
    Steuer *et.al.* 1974)
The Scientific Study of Society (Springer 2003)

Articles

In professional journals (approx. 50)
Other outlets (approx. 40)

Fiction

The Committee (short story)
Film script, with Peter Sykes, for the film The Committee (1968), music by
    Pink Floyd, and a 'Fire' appearance by The Crazy World of Arthur Brown.

Dedicated to
Ken Binmore, mathematician, economist, and philosopher with an eye for the foundations.

and to the memory of
Henry Phelps Brown who possessed a profound appreciation of relevant facts and promoted economic understanding as a vital means of improving public policy.

Preface

After deliberation, I have opted for the male pronoun almost throughout. Old-fashioned no doubt. But to my ear 'she' sounds like you are referring to a particular person. And 'he or she' is cumbersome. I use this last sparingly depending on the context and rhythm of the paragraph.

More to the point, the past 50 years have seen an enormous increase in the number of women studying economics, and there are many more women in university posts in economics, as well as in public policy and economic journalism. Several women hold the most senior posts. This is a very good thing. In my view the gender balance does not change the way economics is done or what is studied. The benefit of having more women comes from having many more extremely able practitioners in the discipline.

In this book I have not used any mathematics, or diagrams, or even references. I believe it is a challenge to tell the tale without using those props. I also expect that sticking to words is more attractive to most non-economist readers.

Contents

About the Author

Max Steuer has been a member of the Economics Department at the London School of Economics (LSE), UK, since 1959, and is a Reader Emeritus in the Economics Department, LSE. He was a Co-Director of the Centre for Philosophy of Natural and Social Science, LSE; and a Programme Associate, at Cities Programme, LSE. Steuer has wide experience. In addition to economics he has taught in the departments of mathematics, sociology, operations research and philosophy. Steuer is now a part time lecturer at LSE. He had extended leaves of absence at the University of Pennsylvania and the University of Ghana. Steuer has published approximately 70 articles in professional journals. Book publications include *Mathematical Sociology* with Janet Holland, *The Impact of Foreign Direct Investment on the United Kingdom*, Steuer et. al. and *The Scientific Study of Society*.

1

Greed and Ignorance

M. Steuer, *Dangerous Guesswork In Economic Policy*,
https://doi.org/10.1007/978-3-031-56078-1_1

At the time of writing this book, the need for better public policy in many countries is there for all to see. Inflation is widespread and persistent. Basic elements of the world economy and national economies like food and energy are under stress. Meeting current needs and at the same time addressing the climate challenge appears to be impossible. Wars in Europe and elsewhere, catastrophic in themselves, have major economic spillovers. Politicians who aspire to more than power, to improving things, face an enormous challenge. Few matters are purely economic, but most issues have an economic element. Recognising that there is knowledge out there is the first step. This is no do-it-yourself job. It calls for expertise. The task of finding a suitable economics adviser is not easy.

Some highly damaging factors have causes which have nothing to do with government policies. Other problems are caused by leaders who put their own interests above those of the country. Ignorance of economic policy is common among world leaders and damages national economies. Better economic policies will not solve all problems, but they can make a bad situation less bad. These grave problems are social and political in nature as well as having economic aspects. Nothing is entirely economic, and nothing is free of economic involvement. This is why it is essential to draw on economic knowledge. The economic aspects of current disasters are complex in the extreme. Serious knowledge is needed. The economic conundrums cannot be addressed by hunches, guesswork, and common sense.

Most economists are highly specialised. There are advantages and disadvantages to specialisation. My career as a researcher and a teacher in economics has been very unspecialised. There is a cost to this approach. A great deal of preparation is needed to publish research findings in leading journals. This must be undertaken afresh with each new topic. The advantage from working in many aspects of the economy is developing an overview of interactions across the economy. The view of economics set out in this book will not be universally agreed by all economists. I present my view and leave it to others to promote their views of economics.

Decision-makers with little economic knowledge face the task of identifying individuals with enough understanding to make a positive contribution. Finding a good economic adviser depends on having an overview of economics. This is critical, and there is no way around it. Simply paying more will not improve the chances of securing a good adviser. Some understanding of the nature of economic knowledge is essential when choosing an adviser. What is economic knowledge? Is it science? Is it reliable? How does it work?

The object of this book is to provide an insightful appreciation of economics. This level of understanding will improve the chances of selecting a good economic adviser. My guided tour of economics is not comprehensive. History of thought is interesting and sometimes revealing. Among other things, it covers historical debates on how to understand and analyse the social activity of producing goods and services and consuming them. It is a pity that the demands of the mathematical training of students leave no time for that pursuit. Nor is it discussed here.

The picture I offer of modern economic thinking and its methods of investigation is highly selective, to the point of being idiosyncratic. This is intentional. Rather than romping through the various specialisms and methods of investigation, I allow the overall nature of this remarkable subject to emerge. My method is to encourage the common elements that underlie all of economics to peak out here and there and eventually reveal the nature of the subject. I offer no apologies for giving my view of the subject rather than a systematic coverage of all the many current conceptions of the subject.

This book is about economic advice, essentially advice of relevance to governments. It is not about financial advice. It will not show the reader how to pay less tax or how to invest his money. That is financial advice. It is something else. This book is about economic advice.

This book offers valuable information to two distinct groups of readers. One group is small, and my publishers are relieved to learn that the other group is large and diverse in nature. The small group consists of heads of state, or highly placed government officials who seek advice on introducing economic policies that will benefit their countries.

It is a harsh fact of life that some heads of state care more about themselves than about their country. The deposed leader of Afghanistan Ashraf Ghani fled the country allegedly clutching millions of dollars in cash that was intended to be used for the benefit of Afghanistan. This is hardly a unique action. Putin is alleged to be one of the richest individuals on the planet, money obtained through running a mafia-style government. He denies having built an elaborate palace for himself. Houphouet-Boigny, a former leader of Ivory Coast, also built a palace for himself, though not on the scale of the Russian's. A smaller indulgence, but perhaps even more damaging to a small population. Erdogan of Turkey is another builder of a private palace.

Massive leaks from law firms, accountants, and banks have been disturbing, providing details of what many suspected all along. First the Panama Papers, then the Paradise Papers, and now the Pandora Papers reveal the staggering level of ill-gotten gains on the part of government officials and their accomplices. Are there any honourable heads of state who need this book? We can only hope so.

The motives of heads of state are complex and vary greatly depending on national customs, geography, and economic circumstances. Hanging on to power is a common objective, along with preparing for the day their rule comes to an end. Feeding a Swiss bank account by diverting public funds is a crude method of self-enrichment. Slightly more subtle is doing favours for corporate and other interests in return for future favourable treatment. Lyndon Johnson rose to be President of the United States from humble beginnings. His wife became wealthy by securing the rights to several broadcasting channels. Whether her bids for those rights were the most competent has been disputed.

Of course, even a leader of a corrupt country may want the economy of his country to perform well. And why not? A thriving economy may enhance the power of the leader. But how to achieve that? A casual glance over the array of countries suggests that in many instances the ruling group is either woefully ignorant of the role and potential contribution of good economic policy or just indifferent to them. Appointing friends, relatives, or supporters to posts of authority on economic matters may appeal to leaders who have concerns other than the economy. Maybe they simply do not realise there is such a thing as expertise in these matters.

Am I too pessimistic? Some leaders must feel that being head of state or in a position of high authority is a profound honour and a great responsibility and is sufficient reward in itself. Looking to the future, they may rightly assume, particularly in the era of celebrity, they need not worry unduly about what will happen to them when they leave office. This book is directed to such individuals, and by default to those who want to have a well-functioning economy. The first step is recognising that these are not simple matters. The task of identifying suitable advisers is not obvious or straightforward. Help is at hand.

In most political setups, there are nominal heads of departments relating to the economy. The economist is a 'backroom' functionary. There are exceptions. Mervyn King, a seriously able economist, was Governor of the Bank of England. Janet Yellen is head of the United States Treasury and is a distinguished economist.

Smaller countries have less elaborate economic establishments. All countries, whether in disarray or not, can benefit from better economic advice. How advisers should be deployed across government is the subject of another book. This book provides a sophisticated overview of economics and the information selectors need to make good choices.

Observing the activity of finding good advisers can be fascinating and sometimes useful to many people not themselves actively involved in this process. I call them bystanders or spectators. What they can glean from being observers is, like the selectors themselves, a sophisticated glimpse into economic understanding.

Reading this book will not make you an economist. That is asking too much. It will give an insight into the activity. Believe it or not, some highly placed economists lack that sophistication. It is possible for researchers to do useful work without understanding the deeper significance of what they are doing. Put another way, they do not appreciate how their work relates to the ongoing structure and application of knowledge. They may feel outrage with that suggestion, and certainly will disagree. I would like this book to promote some interaction with that group but I am not optimistic. They have been doing things in a certain way, have achieved status, and have invested much time and effort. All without reflecting much on what they are doing, so why bother. But you never know.

I would dearly like this book to engage with some people who are thinking about studying economics and perhaps becoming economists. I hope the deliberations to follow will encourage them to do so. Better still, a sophisticated head start will be an advantage in taking on the heavy work that lies ahead for them. It may offer a way around some of the awkward corners that trouble discerning students who want to have a deeper appreciation and understanding of what is going on.

Most current students could also benefit from a little sophistication. In the summer before going to university I read a book which clinched my plan to do economics. When I began my studies, I found it impossible to see the point of some elements of the subject. One aspect of the discipline attempts to understand the behaviour and responses to policy of firms in particular competitive environments. One such environment is called imperfect competition. Firms in this environment have some degree of monopoly power, but much less than a firm who has no direct competitors. Examples of this type of firm might be well-known sports shoe manufacturers or makers of heavily branded food products.

When I was a student there was considerable interest in possible differences between the British and American versions of imperfect competition. I could easily follow the arguments, often carried on in diagrams in those days. The techniques were not difficult. My problem was I could not see the point of this branch of theorising. It was intended to apply equally well to a chain of restaurants and a firm making electric cars. This seemed absurd to me. I found an approachable teacher and confessed I could not see the point of this analysis. Is it remotely realistic? Does this theory relate to a deep truth with wide application? Could you undertake some statistical or other form of investigation to see if the theory fits the facts, and what facts? Or is this theory some kind of fairy tale?

My teacher explained that it was early days, and in time it would make sense to me. More likely he was saying just stop worrying. That is very bad. Understanding should make sense at all levels. I hope this book will encourage a thoughtful and critical approach to learning, but not too critical.

That teacher could have said that he was unsure about the point of that branch of theory. Better still, he could have said that some parts of economics aim at a high level of generality and aim to cover a large category of activities wherever they occur. So only aspects that apply in all cases are considered. The price of the product is one such aspect. Concentrating on what is common to all firms results in an overemphasis on the price a firm set for a product. The analysis proceeds without taking into consideration other decisions and responses such as exactly what type of product to produce and the role of advertising. The United Kingdom Treasury economist Sir Alan Budd and I started some work on the issue of overemphasis on price in economic analysis. Perhaps we should have done more.

On the whole, economic theory is intended to apply to a wide range of economies. The analysis is separate and distinct from other features of the society. This has huge implications for the application of economic knowledge to practical problems. The theory is essential for structuring the analysis, but it must be supplemented with knowledge of particular circumstances. Throughout this book there are many illustrations of the need to supplement received theory with information about the context in which the theory is applied. The relation between highly abstract and universally applicable theory and applied understanding is central to economics. This is not a widely agreed matter. I give my view. It is very much influenced by seeing economics as it can be applied to pressing policy problems.

For many people a hallmark of science is the discovery of general principles with wide applicability. It is a mistake to think that this is essential to scientific activity. It may work in physics, but not in economics and probably not in biology. A grasp of theory is essential for economic investigation, but it is only a starting point. Practical use of economic knowledge requires a detailed understanding of relevant circumstances. Economics can pose challenging mathematical and philosophical issues with no obvious or immediate practical applications. That is fine. But economics has the potential to improve national wellbeing. This is the job of the economic adviser.

2

What Is an Economist?

What Is an Economist?

© The Author(s), under exclusive license to Springer Nature Switzerland AG 2024
M. Steuer, *Dangerous Guesswork In Economic Policy*,
https://doi.org/10.1007/978-3-031-56078-1_2

Harry Johnson was an economist of enormous intellect and boundless energy. In the 1960s and 1970s, he held joint professorships at the University of Chicago and the London School of Economics. While visiting the University of Ghana he decided to give a seminar at the sister University of Cape Coast. The road passes the largest slave exporting fort in West Africa. Approaching near a village, the university-provided chauffeur-driven car hit and killed a goat. The accident broke the headlamp on the driver's side.

The owner of the goat, a local farmer, wanted compensation for the loss of his goat. The university driver wanted compensation for the broken headlamp. Who has the better claim? A legalistic approach to the question would refer to related previous legal decisions, and possibly statute law relating to the use of the highway. The highway in this case was a well-maintained dirt road.

The economist would take a different approach. What would be the cost to the farmer of keeping the highway free of animals, possibly by fencing? What would be the cost to drivers of taking more care and possibly travelling slower? Taking a global position of the entire economy, and if there were no other considerations, the solution that entailed the least cost to the society could be favoured. Of course, there are other considerations such as the relations and rights of the traditional economy as against the drive for development. And there is the relative wealth of the farming community and the universities. Maybe neither party should be compensated, leaving farmers to decide how much effort should go into controlling animals and drivers to decide about their speed and attention. Rather than relying on precedent for the best solution, the economist is inclined to appeal to the costs to the society of different conventions.

I once asked Harry Johnson if there was anything an economist needed to know other than economics. Usually a fast talker, on this occasion he paused for reflection and then replied 'no', there is nothing. This is an odd answer. What about the mathematics of analysis? You could say the mathematics *is* the economics. Yet Akerlof's hugely influential analysis of the second-hand car market and Shelling's telling analysis of segregation in housing involved little mathematics. There are many other examples. But we must grant that mathematics is essential for facilitating analysis of many economic issues.

If you see economics as the analysis of the logic of competitive situations and the stability and lack of it in the aggregate economy, Harry Johnson is broadly right. You can do this important work without looking outside the discipline. Whether you will choose the most significant puzzles to explore is another consideration. But if you see economics as a vital discipline for the analysis of pressing public issues, Harry Johnson was wrong. A central argument of this book, illustrated and discussed in many places, is the need to combine economic knowledge with an appreciation of relevant aspects of the society under investigation.

We could go straight to the punchline and describe the characteristics of a good economic adviser and how to find him or her. This would not be the best approach. It would be like painting by numbers. The decision taker is in a much better position to make a good choice if armed with a basic and hopefully sophisticated understanding of what is an economist, what is an economy, and how economists go about understanding the workings of an economy.

Unlike doctors, lawyers, electricians, and others, there is no professional society or licensing scheme that certifies that someone is an economist. Anyone can claim to be an economist, and this has led to some disturbing results. This section sets out solutions to the practical problem of identifying an economist. That is a minimal objective. The more serious challenge is finding the right adviser among the group of economists. Some highly regarded economists would not make good advisers. Making a better selection will depend on some appreciation of what an economist might do and his approach to the subject.

A head of state fleeing the country by night with a bundle of stolen cash, or anticipating enjoying a well-stocked, if not entirely appropriately acquired, Swiss Bank account does not need an economist. He needs a financial adviser. Advice might be given on how to hide the money, how to launder money, and how to invest. An economist may have some thoughts on some of these matters, but that is by the by.

A crucial distinction between an economist and a financial adviser is that the latter has skills relevant to an individual or particular interests. The economist's skills are relevant to the entire economy. Advancing the interests of a particular group, lawyers for example, may be fine for them but not so good for their clients and for the economy. Of course, promoting the interests of a particular group, the activity of lobbyists, may be consistent with national benefit. Typically, it will not, and in any case the interests of a subgroup of the economy are a different thing from the wellbeing of that great organism the economy.

Efficiency experts in the form of management consultants, or practitioners from the academic discipline operations research, undertake work related, fairly distantly, to that of economists. The London School of Economics hired a consultant who suggested removing the mail deliverer, in the days before mail became electronic, and so save a salary. A later consultant advised creating that post and so saving time the academic staff spent collecting mail. This is a tale of poor advice and later correcting for it.

Economists are also concerned with efficiency, but from a different perspective. A good management consultant may give excellent advice on improving the performance of a call centre or a company switchboard. It seems the advice they give is keep the caller hanging on for a long time. Maybe profitable for the company. Not so good for the caller.

An informed consultant may give excellent advice on improving an assembly line, or how and when to use robots. Do not expect the economist to have much to say of use to farmers, manufacturers, or office teams. Improving the performance of parts of the economy is not the same as improving the performance of the whole system. Economists have a different way of thinking about efficiency, and they have other concerns in addition to efficiency. Later we will address the less than obvious question of what an economy is.

The members of most societies care about some notion of fairness. Economic policy can play a central role in implementing various views of fairness. It also is reasonable, as I will discuss, for a society to care about some degree of self-sufficiency, even at some cost in efficiency. It should be noted and emphasised at this point that economists do not have objectives for society. Social objectives do not come from the discipline of economics. As concerned citizens economists may have views on what is a good society, but that is a personal matter, not derived from the subject economics. Economists are facilitators. You tell me what you want, and I'll tell you how to achieve it.

This last assertion screams out for qualification. Individuals in a society, and in some sense the general will of the society, if there is such a thing, may have no clear idea of what they want. They want things to be better, whatever that might mean. In this sense the task of the economist is ill-defined. That does not mean one opinion is as good as another. We will have some discussion of ways of dealing with ill-defined objectives.

The economist is also better placed than most observers to appreciate the fuller implications of different policy objectives. Some welfare schemes may have what I would call the worthy objective of improving the lot of the poor. In fact, they may do that inefficiently and even be counterproductive. Understanding the interconnections of the economy and spotting unintended implications of economic policies is at the centre of the economists' expertise.

The economist has an edge in tracing out the effects of policies and better ways of achieving desired ends. But at bottom, the goals of society are for the collective to determine. Really? Do people really know what they want, what they take to be right, and what they believe? Often the economist can contribute more by avoiding bad outcomes that nobody wants but did not see coming.

It worries me sometimes when economists sign petitions, for example opposing budgetary austerity, as if they have clinching arguments they derive from their knowledge of economics. They may have some pretty good points to make about long-run and more immediate effects, and who is bearing most of the cost of austerity. But ultimately the objectives of society come from elsewhere, not from economics.

A similar situation arises with policies to deal with the pandemic. Policymakers say they are following the science. But no amount of medical science can tell you whether to have a lockdown. The science is relevant to informed decision-making. But the ultimate basis of any such decision comes from out++side science.

No doubt the previous paragraph is a little simplistic. I do not want to drift too far into philosophical concerns from which we may never return. But we do need to devote some attention to the economist's view of consumer preferences and the choices consumers make when they buy things. Generally, economists adopt a hands-off view of consumer choice.

If that is what people want, so to be it. Policy should aim at expanding the range of choice, a widely agreed position. Some extreme advocates of consumer sovereignty would place no impediments to addiction to hard drugs, or the activities of prostitutes. Some more moderate economists do not object to legislation which reduces the amount of sugar in soft drinks. This and related policy initiatives are regarded as exceptions to the general rule that consumers should be free to choose, even if their choices are in some sense mistaken or possibly harmful to themselves. Economists are opposed to choices that harm others.

Such views, while popular among economists, do not follow from anything in economics. They come from values and preferences. Economists also tend to favour consumer sovereignty for reasons that have nothing to do with consumer welfare. Leaving choices up to consumers can simplify the analysis of economic issues. Economists do not always recognise this. If you believe that expanding choice is always a good thing and more important than other objectives, it follows that promoting the growth of the economy above all else is a good thing. Growth of the economy appears to be especially important for poor countries. And so it might be. It is another matter if the possibilities of economic growth actually bring benefits to the poor.

A simple-minded view of growth risks ignoring issues of environmental damage and other considerations. Some say, rightly in principle but doubtful in practice, that it is a matter of having the right measure of growth. But even if growth is properly measured and accounted for, the discipline of economics does not support growth policies, however popular they are with governments and the populace generally. Should we do more to improve what goes on in prisons, or should we have better roads? Let's have more economic growth, then we can do both. Wrong. No feasible amount of growth can avoid decisions about allocation. The growth fetish disguises and puts off difficult decisions.

Economists can have a lot of useful things to say about economic growth and how to achieve it. As individuals they may have preferences and values regarding the importance of growth. As economists they can only tell you how things work, cause and effect, but not what to do. For some the very word 'economics' implies a mean spirited, materialistic sort of person. An economist must be someone who cares about money more than about truth or love. Not so! If you have a view about what is a just or fair society, an economist can have useful things to say about how to achieve it. An economist is a social scientist, a person who studies and attempts to understand how an aspect of society works. What is an economist? An economist is a person who studies economies.

So far so good. However, as we point out, economists are not licensed. Anyone can call themselves an economist. They may have little training in the subject or even none at all. Some fakers pretend to education they do not have. This is common, as is the claim that no formal education is needed. Common sense and wide experience are enough, and are superior to book learning and academic knowledge, or so the claim goes. This is a big issue. It comes up in several sections below. I think it is wrong. The reader must decide. The section on the nature of economics as a discipline is particularly relevant to an informed decision.

A self-styled economist is one thing. A highly trained professional is something else. In the latter sense, an economist is someone with a Ph.D. degree from a well-recognised university. The club of economists knows a member when they see one. The Ph.D. is the minimum requirement. Other indicators signal superior standing, such as significant research publications.

This section is essentially definitional. It answers the question 'what is an economist?' The answer has several aspects. The key feature is a social scientist who studies economies, not from a historical or sociological perspective, but in terms of how economies work, what causes what. This definition begs the question, "what is an economy?" Standard teaching rather takes it for granted that the answer is obvious. It is not obvious, as we shall see.

3

The Economy and the Many Economies

The distinguished economist Georgescu-Rogan accepted an invitation to visit the Economics Department at the University of Ghana. He explained that he had never been to Africa and was keen to learn something about West Africa. Within hours of the drive from the airport, he gave a seminar on life in a Ghanaian village. His topic surprised the teachers as did the many nods of recognition from the student audience. After the seminar we asked Professor Georgescu-Rogan how he managed to display such insight.

He explained that he had done research on peasant life in Eastern Europe. He assumed that much the same features applied to Ghanaian village life. The gamble proved correct. The two most important common features are, firstly, that the economy, the system of consumption and production, was almost entirely organised by the extended family unit.

The second feature is that these economic units are largely self-sufficient. Occasionally some casual labour is hired during intense periods of planting and harvesting. This is limited in scope. Typically, the outside labour is paid in cash and is not part of the family pattern of consumption. There also is a small amount of trade between the extended family village and the wider economy. Some food and a few other products are sold and some additional cash is earned through brief periods of paid work undertaken away from the village. Money earned buys a few imports from outside. The dominant pattern of the village economy is self-sufficiency.

This extended family economy is not a market economy in the conventional sense. Senior figures assign work in food production, shelter building, and looking after children. Few actual orders are given as convention determines the activities of individuals. The output is distributed to family

© The Author(s), under exclusive license to Springer Nature Switzerland AG 2024
M. Steuer, *Dangerous Guesswork In Economic Policy*,
https://doi.org/10.1007/978-3-031-56078-1_3

members along lines the family and its leaders deem to be equitable, again, largely determined by custom and convention.

Clearly this economy, the system of production and consumption, is intimately embedded in the society. The family leaders control the economy. The economy and the society were as one. This is not a very productive form of economy. Self-sufficiency and the lack of a significant degree of specialisation necessarily mean a low level of production.

There are features of this kind of society which many would find attractive. Children relate to a wider circle of adults than in the more modern nuclear family. The sense of community and pleasure in the community is strong. Members are secure against falling below the village standard. Old age may lack some of the comforts of a care home, but the life of the old is likely to be more meaningful in the village.

Just as an aside, the outside world sees this as a less developed economy, and to some extent the village members accept the concept of living in a system that is unsatisfactory and will change. Yet change is hard to achieve, however much it may be welcomed in the abstract. Part of the reason is that you cannot modernise a single village on its own. The wider economy has to change. Another concern is that a different economy will entail different social relations. The transition can be hurtful, and no obvious alternative system is out there waiting to be adopted. This is a complex story, and enough on it for now.

While modern life is very different, the economy, the system of production of goods and services and the claims people have on the output, is still intimately embedded in the society. Even conceptually we cannot say where the economy ends and the rest of society takes over. Marriage prospects and social life generally are involved in numerous connections with economic activity and the economy. The economy is a major factor in social status. The labour market, for example, is not something outside the wider social system.

Community values and what is fair and appropriate influence the functioning of the economy. Some societies can live happily, or at least acceptingly, with leaders of large firms earning 300 times that of average employees rather than 30 times as in past years. Nick Clegg, the former leader of the Liberal Party, leaves politics and takes a job at Facebook eventually earning over 20 million pounds a year. This is accepted in the United Kingdom. Other societies reject this level of remuneration. The degree and nature of inequality influences the society as well as the culture and values of society affecting inequality.

Some scholars have suggested that a prosperous and well-functioning economy is promoted by, and perhaps even dependent on, respect for the individual, liberal values, and freedom. They claim that China is a temporary aberration. Karl Marx took the opposite view. His claim is the economy or the relations of production to use Marxist terminology determine the nature of society. The dominant causality runs one way according to Marx. The productive system determines the class system, the bedrock of society. The liberal view that economic success and the nature of the economy are determining factors disagrees with the Marxist view. Both of these views are mistaken.

It would be much easier to understand what is going on, and as a result be easier to formulate effective policies, if the relation between the economy and the wider society was a one-way street, a one-way street in either direction—society determining the economy, or the economy determining the society. Einstein said you should make your analysis as simple as possible but not simpler. As it happens, the causal relations between the economy and the society are multiple, are complex, and run in all directions.

My claim is that the economy is more involved with the society than just setting the tone. It influences the nature of the society. And in turn, the nature of the society feeds back on the economy. I can hear a winner of a Nobel Prize in economics who I will not name saying, 'Can you model that?' The challenge is to write down a set of mathematical equations that capture at least one possible version of these interconnections. I cannot, right now. But I can provide compelling examples.

John Maynard Keynes was one of the few truly great economists. When he retired from editing *The Economic Journal,* he made a speech which troubled me when I first read it and still upsets me. How can such an able thinker hold such an absurd view? I put it politely. I think he was profoundly wrong.

Keynes said the economy is unimportant. It is like the plumbing of a house. It should not leak. It should be quiet and efficient. But that is all. What is important is the life being lived in the house. The error is to assume the economy is something distinct from peoples' lives.

As I have tried to indicate above, the kind of economy we have is both influenced by the kind of society we have and crucially influences that society. The economy is not something working away, efficiently or otherwise, in the background. The economy is integral to the society.

And where are the borders? Where does the economy end and something else begin? We have gone quite far without saying what is an economy, other than a few phrases about producing things and distributing them among the populace. We can go further.

A lot of economic theory implicitly suggests that the economy is the market. The bulk of economic theory does not refer to a particular country or a particular period. That is fine for certain purposes. As will be developed further below, it means that employing theory involves additional considerations.

Even in a predominantly market economy, the economy is much wider than the market. Everyone knows that the government does things, that charitable agencies operate, that work is done in households, and so on. The market is not all, and markets differ widely one from another in nominally capitalist countries.

Can you take a group of people on a field trip to observe the economy? It depends on what you mean. We certainly can show people buying stuff in a shop or online. We could show farmers growing food, or robots and people making electric cars. But that might be taking place in a command economy like the old Russia. Or it might be Japan today. Do they have the same kind of economy? Certainly not. The field trip does not work as a way of observing the economy because the economy is the system of arrangements that links the vast array of activities involved in making things and providing goods and services across the society. We might take a group to observe life in a communist country like North Korea or China. We would be observing specific practices, not the economic system that, along with other factors, coordinates activities. The focus in this book is on the system, partly rules and partly custom, for undertaking production and distribution.

This focus is in line with economic analysis generally. There are important exceptions. But we usually assume that the parts that make up the system are operating reasonably according to their objectives. Consumers are spending their money in a sensible way and production units are operating effectively. So what more is needed?

Even if we have little to say about the parts and their efficacy, the system may have weaknesses, sometimes serious weaknesses. There may be too many firms in a particular industry and competition may be slow in removing some. Investment and innovation may be sub-optimal because of the incentive elements of the economic system. Patents and interest rates may be giving the wrong signals to producers just to mention two factors.

Taxation is a third vital consideration. What is taxed, how it is taxed, and the rate of taxation can do a good job of raising necessary revenue with minimal harm to the economy, or taxation policy may be poorly organised. How much tax revenue is optimal is another consideration beyond the reach of consumer and producing units. Similar remarks can be made about managing the money system. The economy can go off the rails and generate tragic levels of unemployment or hugely damaging inflation. There is much to do about the economy even if the parts function well. In addition, the functioning of the parts is influenced by the rules and customs of the system and by economic policy.

We speak about the economy of a country. Is there a problem here? Italy has a prosperous North and a less affluent South. In the United Kingdom it is the other way around. Is there one economy in each country or two economies? We could make other divisions: a rural economy and an urban one, a service economy and a manufacturing one, and so on.

Some governments express a wish to 'level up' regional differences in economic prosperity. The United Kingdom policy initiative of 'levelling up' stands a good chance of appealing to the voters. The well-off will not lose and the less well-off will gain. What could be better? How to achieve this transformation? No problem says the government official. It cannot be done without transferring resources from the better-off regions to the less well-off areas, says the economist. Who will the government listen to?

Economies are linked through trade, capital movements, and migration. In what sense is there a national economy, an economy of the United Kingdom or Ethiopia? Some economies are reasonably homogeneous in economic level and economic practice. But some are more like two or more different economies, one poor and another wealthy and modern. And the economic activity of a country involves other economies.

A good reason to think of the nation state, a geographic area, as an economy is because of decision-making. The government of the nation state can determine policies for the national economy. The government does not have complete control over policies. Action taken in other countries will have effects. But in addition to a somewhat common language, a somewhat common culture, and relative freedom of movement within the country, government policy is predominant within the geographic area of a national economy. There is a world economy, but no world policymakers. This has consequences we will explore.

Thomas Piketty has argued that economics, the study of the economies, is too separate, too independent from the rest of social enquiry. He is right. The training of economists and the vast bulk of economic theory and analysis treat economies as if they were distinct from the rest of society. We will return to this problem and what to do about it when we explore the methods and practices of economics as a social science. These issues are important considerations for a successful economic adviser.

Closely related to the separateness of economic analysis from social relations is the question of the kind of economy a country has. All economies are mixed in the sense that market forces play a role, government activity and government decisions play a role, and informal, if not illegal, activity, or what some people might call the grey or black market, plays a role. In many economies the market is dominant, and we classify them as capitalist or market economies. Yet the variation between market economies is huge. The United States is not the same as the United Kingdom or South Korea. Again economic theory tends to ignore these differences. There are good reasons and potentially bad consequences of this way of doing things. The mystery deepens. The unsophisticated economist, however technically skilled, ignores these complications. That may be alright for an academic researcher. But not for advising on policy.

This section is a start to answering the question, what is an economy? It is a system relating multitudes of parts. The key concept is the system, not the parts. The borders between one economy and another are not sharp or distinct. They are fuzzy borders, to use popular language. And the borders between what is an economy and what are other aspects of society are also fuzzy. Physicists and biologists study things which in important respects are not changing. A hydrogen atom is the same today as it was years ago. A mouse is much the same. An economy is likely to be different.

Economies are changing. People change their behaviour as they have new experiences, or a great deal of repetition of familiar experiences. The way things are made and what is made change over time. The customs, rules, and practices of economic engagement change. This loosely defined and changing entity is what economists study. Others also have views on economic matters. A close look at economics as a discipline of enquiry reveals features of the economic perspective.

4

Kinds of Advisers

Economists tend to infer people's motives, goals, and objectives from what they do, the actions they take, rather than from what they say. In many cases nothing is said, but a reasonable guess about what people believe can be deduced from their observed behaviour. On that basis we might conclude that many governments believe that economic policy is unimportant or is a matter of common sense not calling for specialised knowledge or both. The evidence for this conclusion is the economic advisers they appoint.

Many governments have non-economic advisers or no advisers. Political appointments are doled out based on positions in the ruling structure and on little else. I hope that the discussion of what is an economy and some brief indications of what might be done to shape and direct the economy are sufficient grounds for rejecting this approach. Trusting to luck with an institution of such importance to material wellbeing and to the nature of the society is foolhardy. Any justification along the lines that the economy is self-adjusting, is functioning optimally, or near optimally is ideology gone mad. It amounts to placing faith above reasoning.

A completely different approach recognises both the importance and challenging difficulties of managing the economy effectively, or at least not disastrously. At the time of writing, a rampant inflation is causing turmoil and suffering in the United Kingdom and elsewhere. Monetary authorities have a lot to answer for. This criticism is not based on the wisdom of hindsight. It is based on failing to act on the basis of information known at the time. Reducing the money supply and damping down the level of economic activity could have been undertaken.

M. Steuer, *Dangerous Guesswork In Economic Policy*,
https://doi.org/10.1007/978-3-031-56078-1_4

An alternative approach recognises the problem of managing the economy but holds that economists are not the best people to deal with it. A significant body of opinion maintains that businesspeople, people with hands-on experience of the economy and successful careers in business, are better placed to offer advice than economists who have only academic knowledge.

The word 'only' loads the debate in two ways. It suggests that academic knowledge is not real knowledge, the ivory tower and all that. It also suggests that economists are confined to the classroom and research centres and have restricted views of the world. Well, this is true of many economists, but not of those economists we might choose as advisers.

Another aside to the reader is in order. I refer to something obvious. This discussion is undertaken by someone with a lifetime in economic teaching, research, and some advising. It would be prudent to be a little sceptical and to be on guard against bias in the presentation. Be sceptical, no problem. We all have histories and come from somewhere. The important thing is listening and taking on board the arguments.

The old phrase, what is good for General Motors is good for the country, encapsulates the view that businesspeople are the best advisers. Most of this discussion will address that position. Lowering the minimum wage and relaxing pollution regulations might be good for General Motors, but will it be good or bad for the country?

A small group favours advisers with proven high levels of intelligence, very high levels, regardless of profession. Could an economist fall into that group? It has been suggested by a distinguished economist that economics has not had the benefit of a great mind. I will give a short response, just to wrap this up. Great minds prefer to work on difficult but definitively solvable problems. Ultimately these are well-defined problems. Many economic problems are ill-defined and call for different kinds of ability. If you want to call one ability superior to another, I have no problem with that because I do not care about it.

Taking first the more widely supported and to me the plausible claim that businesspeople will make better advisers than economists, I take it that we do not mean just any experienced businessperson. The more plausible position is that success in business shows serious understanding of the workings of the economy. Three issues arise. In many cases it is surprisingly difficult to identify success. Secondly, is there a general ability for business success regardless of the nature of the business? And finally, does success in business give evidence of how to apply economic policies?

I begin with what might be taken to be a digression. Increasingly, but maybe it always was the case, a huge amount of crookery and vile behaviour goes on in business. Bankrupt firms are bought for a song in order to acquire the pension fund and steal it away from the workers. Allowing this is a failure of governments, and it is a mystery to me why so little is done about it.

Recently in the United Kingdom all water providing authorities were privatised and their debts written off. Generally, the CEOs and the senior staff of these new entities receive very large compensation packages compared to compensation when the activity was in the public sector. Shareholders have done well. Dumping untreated sewage into rivers and the ocean has escalated. Underinvestment and a great deal of borrowing have gone hand in hand. Eventual bankruptcy will be a problem for the lenders, but not for the CEOs with lush retirement levels of assets. Some even go on to head up other firms. Is the business world good at choosing business leaders, let alone acting as a source of economic advisers?

Final accounting is yet to be done, but there are grounds for suspecting that lucrative contracts for pandemic-related needs were let to unqualified and some almost non-existent firms in the United Kingdom, who failed to deliver. If true, it is a failure of government, but with willing participation from the business world. I mention all this not to bash business, but to suggest that business orientation is to special interests, not to the general interest, and can cross the line into corruption.

Villainy is one thing, but even honest achievement is hard to discern. A study of executives of oil companies shows that profits, as a measure of success, have little to do with executive decisions and everything to do with the price of oil, over which they have no control. Quite conceivably a CEO of a seriously declining firm might have made brilliant decisions that avoided even greater loss. It is not easy to identify success in business.

Headhunting firms generally agree that the high remuneration of business leaders in the United States, the United Kingdom, and elsewhere is not due to a shortage of suitable talent. Quite the contrary. The pool of potential candidates is large. Securing a post has more to do with an acceptable career path, luck, and fitting in with corporate culture.

There are many exceptions, of course. My personal view is that Bill Gates would make an excellent economic adviser. He had an insight into computing that seems to have eluded the directors of IBM. He combined his insight with extraordinary business acumen. He also threw massive legal resources at attempts to curb monopoly power. From what little I know about Bill Gates I think he would make an outstanding economic adviser, not because of his business ability, but because he would assemble a talented group of economists, coordinate their efforts, and promote their findings.

This last speculation slightly muddies the waters. This discussion has to do with a businessperson as a preferred alternative to an economist. I mention

IBM. But the track record of leaders of major firms who failed to respond to changes in their sectors is legion. Kodak, Bethlehem Steel, and Woolworths come to mind. Businesspeople can be very stuck in their ways, but no doubt not all of them.

A former director of the Chrysler corporation strongly questioned the belief that there is such a thing as general business ability. To convey an air of leadership, commanding respect and convening panels of senior specialists is common to much of business. But will a good leader of a restaurant chain also be a good leader of an electric car firm?

Success in business usually has a lot to do with finding a niche or dealing with the competition. Good decisions depend on instinct and knowledge of a sector. Broader issues like taxation, regulation, labour market practices, and the like are important in so far as they impinge on the particular sector. Their role and importance in the wider economy is a secondary consideration for the business leader.

For many firms success is related to predicting and appreciating broader changes and trends in the wider economy. Repeated ability in this regard would indicate skill in some aspects of the task of economic adviser. Just a single success is a weaker indicator. Observing, predicting, and appreciating trends in fashion and in consumer preferences is different from predicting unemployment or economic growth. The core activity of the economic adviser is appreciating where action is needed and predicting the consequences of economic policies. This is important and under-appreciated. Often spotting a problem involves observing, not predicting. For undertaking policy moves, predicting the consequences of policy interventions is primary.

No doubt business experience has a bearing. We have to choose an economic adviser. Who do we want? An economist, the right economist, or someone from the business world, the right businessperson. It is a cop-out to say let's have a team. A business adviser could draw on economists, and an economist as adviser could draw on business knowledge. Which is likely to be more effective in seeking information?

An alternative to the economist or the businessperson is simply to go for brains. Why not take the smartest physicist or mathematician as economic adviser? Here we have some experience to draw on. Several representatives from this august group have looked at the mathematics used in economic analysis and felt that they could do much better. The economics profession is surprisingly open to such suggestions. Have a go. No problem. Come back when you have something.

Most never come back. Some come back with nonsense. Being intelligent rational figures, they quickly see how they went wrong when it is pointed out to them. Very few come back for a second try. If they do, they tend to change profession and become economists. Some are quite good economists, but not distinguishable from those who enter the profession from conventional channels.

The central consideration in deciding whether to choose an economist, a businessperson, or someone from any other group is the nature of economic knowledge. Is it just common sense writ large? Do economic theories give reliable accounts of the workings of economies? Is economic theory applied in a straightforward, almost mechanical way? Or must the theory be supplemented with other means of understanding? A sensible choice of an economist or someone else depends on what economists have to offer. And that depends in large part on the discipline of economics.

The distinction between business as usual and an economy experiencing significant shocks calls for comment. The economy is continually changing, so even a society with what is agreed to be a good working economy will require tinkering at the edges. Small mistakes may have limited consequences, but they can cumulate. Natural or man-made disasters, like a financial crisis, can benefit enormously from accurate diagnoses, forecasting, where possible, and skilled firefighting in any case.

We tend to think of economics as dealing with troubles. What about a large change for the better? What we want is a sustained boom, an economic renaissance. Can economic policy deliver a sustained rise in productivity and growing prosperity? The evidence suggests that an economic renaissance is rather like a cultural renaissance, great when you have one. We probably know more about how bad decisions can discourage a renaissance than bring one about.

Populist politics tends to the view that we have had enough of experts, except for the expertise of the populist leader. Possible justifications are many. The problems are easy and common sense will do. The club of experts is self-justifying and in fact they know no more than anyone else. The expert is like the person who claims to know the will of God. In this discussion I am dismissing such views as nonsense and asking instead what kind of expert? Do we want an economist or someone else?

Specialist knowledge that will help one supermarket increase its market share and profitability at the expense of another supermarket is most unlikely to come from an economist. Economic knowledge relates to the system or country as a whole. How well does the economy perform in meeting the needs of the country?

The very notion of the needs of the country, in contrast to the net worth of a firm, is an ambiguous and elusive objective. Economists think a lot about how to sum up the interests of the members of a society into a single objective. The implications of various ways of adding up or aggregating the wellbeing of individuals into a single function are studied usually in rather abstract terms. When there is rough agreement on the objectives of an economy the economist can assess the policy options for getting as far as possible up the mountain of objectives. In principle at least the focus is clear. The economy as a whole and the wellbeing of the members of the society is the object of study.

The use of the term 'wellbeing' is a bit of a cop-out here, something of a weasel word. It allows for a materialistic interpretation but allows for wider interpretations. Some countries, or at least the leadership in those countries, may believe that playing a larger role on the world stage at some cost to consumers is a worthwhile trade-off. Other societies may see restricting the role of women, with its attendant economic cost, as coming closer to the will of God, and therefore worthwhile.

Economists have training and some facility in addressing the functioning of the economy as a whole. The relations between abstract and practical considerations of these matters are taken up in the next section. Present purposes emphasise the contrast between particular interests and the concerns of the society and its economy. Well, that may be the objective, but how successful are economists at understanding the economy?

We are not dealing with certainties here. We are dealing with the probability of choosing a good economic adviser. It could be that a well-spoken, well-dressed businessman or mathematician will give excellent economic advice. This is more likely as a one-off event than a sustained performance. There is no escaping the need to have a pretty good idea about economics if one is to judge well in choosing an adviser. Knowing more about economics will not necessarily lead to choosing an economist as an adviser. But it might. Some knowledge of what economics is about is needed. The next extended section takes up that challenge.

5

The Scope and Methods of Economics

The Scope and Methods of Economics

Economics is a social science along with the four other major social sciences, anthropology, political science, social psychology, and sociology. These subjects, or disciplines, have the shared objective of improving our understanding of aspects of society. It makes some sense to divide up the search for understanding this way, provided we recognise that the subjects shade into each other. There are no clear borders. Social science shares with natural science, physics, biology, and so on the common objective of improving understanding.

Do the social sciences employ the same methods and are they as successful as the natural sciences? Mostly not. We do the best we can, and progress is hard to come by. Social scientists, including economists, face some difficult challenges that do not trouble natural scientists. These problems and the methods used to get around them are explored in this lengthy and critical chapter. Even small gains in understanding the workings of the economy can bring significant benefits.

Many economists are trained in what might be called mainstream methods and approaches. They go on to make use of these methods and approaches in the research they undertake and in applying economics to policy problems facing national governments. The most common of these problems are called stability issues. Economists aim to reduce the harmful effects on individuals and on society of fluctuations, sometimes called the business cycle, and attendant issues of inflation and unemployment. The financial sector of the economy can also be prone to stability issues.

Another great area of investigation in economics is the relation between the government and the economy, involving questions of taxation and regulation. Some say the less regulation and taxation the better. Economists aim to bring some reasoning and evidence to bear on these and related issues. A scientific approach to these issues is in stark contrast to approaches rooted in ideology.

My discussion gives centre stage to mainstream economics, or what is also called neoclassical economics, for no good reason. This dominant approach to economics is what is studied in leading universities and is enshrined in major graduate textbooks. Some attention is given here to the question, what is the current state of knowledge in economics? What is generally agreed to be our current understanding of economies? My focus here on the mainstream does not imply that there is only one approach to gaining economic understanding. Quite the contrary. Almost every conceivable approach has been tried, and in some distant corners many are still being pursued. These minority approaches include large-scale simulation; drawing mainly on historical experiences; and concentrating on complexity as a defining feature of economies.

It is to the credit of the economics profession that we keep an open mind to other approaches. If something works, we are very pleased. We also keep an eye out for crackpot approaches. Some current attempts to apply physics to economics fall into this category. But the dominant approach is the mainstream approach and that is what is described below.

A large amount of economic research is devoted to refining economic theory and developing new theories. Economic policy, the work of the economic adviser, is usually carried on under some time pressure. Rarely is there an opportunity to devise new theory. Informed policy draws on existing theory. This is not done in a simple mechanical way. Theory is essential, but it has to be adapted to prevailing circumstances. What happens when we undertake a policy intervention in the economy depends on the changing features of the system and on the multitude of decisions and actions undertaken by people in the economy. People change with experience and circumstances. Insight into how economists work with changing conditions to arrive at policy conclusions follows.

Reading this chapter is not a substitute for an economics education. Instead, it provides insight into how economists think, and what they do, and how they apply knowledge. Surprisingly, more than a few practitioners of economics get overly wrapped up in the demanding technology of the discipline and might benefit from, and even enjoy, thinking about what they are doing. Economics can be interesting in itself without reference to how economic theory might be used to improve policy.

I am all for so-called pure research. This is partly because it can be exciting, when not devoted to polishing and refinement. And more because ideas developed only for their inherent interest occasionally turn out to have practical applications. This discussion of economics emphasises the contribution it can make to economic policy.

1   Theories and Facts

Any discussion of science, be it natural or social, requires a basic understanding of the concepts of theory and of facts. There is so much confusion and misunderstanding about science. No doubt the readers of this text have a clear understanding of these matters, but for the record and to agree on a common use of terms, a few key points need spelling out.

You often hear from creationists that evolution is just a theory. This is a confused use of language. A theory is an explanation. Scientists of all stripes call their explanations theories. A theory may provide a very comprehensive, accurate, and reliable account of something, or it may be weak in several respects, and, to put it boldly, it may simply be wrong.

Of course, evolution is a theory. It explains how the many living creatures, including us, came to be here. What the creationists could say is that evolution is the wrong theory. The correct theory is stated in the Bible, namely, the Garden of Eden. Or they might say that evolution is a highly speculative theory with little evidence to support it. They would be wrong to say that, but it would be a linguistically meaningful statement.

More reliable theories are not facts. They are better explanations. Facts are observations, things which theories try to explain. Assertions of fact, like it always rains on my birthday, or the earth is getting warmer, may or may not be correct. It gets a little tricky when we think about facts as statements about the world, or alternatively as observations. "When dipped in liquid, this paper turned blue" is a correct report if indeed that is what happened. If we agree how we are using the terms, no problem. Facts, like theories, may be right or wrong.

Early astronomers thought they observed canals on Mars. They were mistaken. Early measurements of the bending of light passing large celestial bodies were wrong. We try to get the theories right and we try to get the facts right. There is no ironclad method for doing either.

Scientific explanations in economics, or in chemistry for that matter, are not standalone propositions. They are parts of a structure of theory, a whole body of understanding. Or, put another way, they are parts of a system of interlocking explanations. This system or structure is not neat, or tidy, or self-consistent. Part of scientific work consists of trying to rationalise the explanatory structure. Some elements of the theory, once held to be necessary, may turn out to be redundant, or unnecessary, as they are manifest in other parts of the theoretical system of explanations. It often takes considerable skill to show that.

If parts of the structure of the theory are inconsistent with other parts, this poses a challenge to scientists and often is helpful in identifying where to look and how to go about improving the theoretical structure. Theories rarely mesh with the facts perfectly. When the mismatch gets too great we reach a point where the search is needed for a new theory.

My last preliminary observation before discussing the practice of economics relates to the notion of laws. Traditionally we call some theories laws. These tend to be theories where we have a lot of confidence that the theory accounts for the facts very well, or the theory has widespread implications, or both. Nothing much is gained by calling some parts of the structure of explanations laws. I suggest dropping this practice, or simply seeing it as a historical practice, like identifying some theories with the name of a particular individual.

What we have in science is explanations and observations. Both may be reasonably reliable, or wrong and misleading. Scientific progress involves identifying and getting rid of bad theories and incorrectly perceived facts. New theories start out as guesses, or speculations, or conjectures. How well they deal with the facts and how well they mesh in with the existing theoretical structure influences their acceptance. Enough of preliminaries.

2   Waste Land Becomes Valuable

Henry George was an economist working during the nineteenth century. He was the last of the significant self-taught economists. Since then, they all come out of university. There is just too much cumulative knowledge for a person not exposed to that knowledge to come up with something new and useful. But you never know. George was concerned with nature as a contributing factor in economic production. We find and extract oil, but we did not put the oil there. That is the contribution of nature. We may hunt and kill whales and extract oil or meat, a mistaken activity in my view, but hard work, nevertheless. We do the work, build the whaling ships which we call capital, and nature provides the whales. We clear land for farming and house building. Nature provides the land.

Much of nature goes its own way, and much of nature is owned by someone or some interest. There are conventions and laws which legitimise private ownership. This is my land. That is your coal under the ground. Current debates are going on about private ownership of space. Who owns the moon? Who has the right to launch satellites?

Henry George was not so much interested in how parts of nature come to be privately owned by an individual or an institution. His concern is with the economic consequences of this private ownership of nature, and what alternative arrangements might be possible, and might produce better results.

George invites us to consider the following thought experiment. He asks us to imagine a large plain crisscrossed by a north-south road and an east-west road. Nothing much is there at the time, but we know, somehow, that in 30 years' time a thriving community will exist where the two roads cross. How might we benefit from this knowledge? Would we plan to move our garage business or hairdressing salon there? No. Why should they do particularly well in this new community compared to elsewhere? We would buy the land, assuming we could set aside a small amount of money for 30 years, and a small investment would eventually become a fortune. This, says George, is not right. We contributed nothing to the development of the community and wound up wealthy. Is he right?

Perhaps we could dig a little deeper. Suppose we do not know there will be a city, town, or whatever at what is now an empty crossroads. We take a punt. We might win or lose it all if nothing develops. Alternatively, as the community develops an opportunity arises to sell off some of the land. How much should we sell? The initial price will be low. If we refuse to sell, will there ever be a community? It is a complex dynamic story.

Critical to that story is whether there is one, a few, or many investors. Maybe several initial investors bought up parcels of land around the crossroads. No doubt there is money to be made here, but how much? With uncertainty about how large and how prosperous the ensuing community will be, one can get into the land market here and make money or lose money.

Right from the beginning there will be interactions between the land market and local government. The market requires rules of engagement. The area may be organised in blocks set up by a consortium of investors, or by a hastily formed community council. Zoning laws may emerge. No noisy production here, no drinking establishments there. Who will pay for the urban regulations and enforcing the laws?

We can postulate that the government parcels out the land to interested individuals at a modest fee. It enforces their contractual right to the land. In addition to the fee, we might imagine that the government retained a continuing interest in the form of an annual charge of 5% on the rental value of the land. George certainly would have favoured that. There is a problem here. The land is one thing, and the structure built on it is something else. The 5% refers to the land only. How do we determine the value of the land as against that of the structure?

Let's step back a moment and ask what is going on here? We are exploring an imaginary tale, usually called a thought experiment. What are the alternatives? If we want to know what happens to land values, to land use, and to demographic dispersion, we could look at the history of other city developments. Nothing wrong with that. But more is needed. No two developmental histories are the same. And simply looking at history will not tell us what caused what. That is where economics comes in, theories about what we come to observe.

Our discussion of the city at the crossroads came up with two conclusions: land prices will rise substantially beyond what they were before the city developed; the return on other activities like running garages or restaurants will be similar to the returns in the country generally. This is pretty much common sense. Being more formal in our analysis, we could derive these two conclusions from two propositions. One is that land is in fixed supply. A little qualification is needed. We are referring to land in the neighbourhood of the city centre. Moving out to the land on the periphery gets cheaper and eventually becomes close to a free good. The land price depends on supply and demand. That is a theory. As demand for land closer to the centre rises, the price will rise.

The second part, about the return on productive activity, rests on competition. Entrepreneurs may head to the new development in the hopes of finding new opportunities. They may well succeed with that, perhaps earning more than they did elsewhere. Initially this community is a harsh place with little medical service and scant entertainment. But the premium for working in a tougher place can only go so high. Eventually, if the extra return is high enough, more entrepreneurs will be drawn in keeping the returns closer to the national average. That is a theory about competition. Two bits of theory can be employed to inform our thought experiment. When the analysis gets more complicated, making things formal and explicit gets more important.

This discussion began with thinking about nature as a factor of production. If no individual or interest owns an aspect of nature, what is known as the problem of the commons arises. If anyone can graze sheep on common land, destructive overgrazing is likely. If anyone can fish in certain waters, overfishing is likely. Some form of ownership is needed to prevent the problem of the commons. It need not be private ownership.

Outer space is a developing example of the problem of free entry. Who owns the moon? The United States planted a flag there. One hopes this was to celebrate the achievement and to discourage others from claiming ownership. If anyone can put up a satellite, eventually there will be too many up there and cascading collisions will occur. It is time now to insure the common ownership of space, perhaps through the United Nations.

3   Wages and Information

Before Alaska became a state, much employment there was seasonal summer work. Heavy demand for labour was driven partly by military spending in the territory. An interesting two-year cycle emerged in this economy. One year a smaller number of workers make the journey to Alaska. Jobs are easy to find, and the pay is high. Rumours of the high pay spread, and the next year many more make the journey. As a result, pay in that year is low. Rumours of low pay spread. Few workers make the journey the next year, and a high pay season ensues, and so on. This cycle is driven by rumour. Expectations are an important consideration in much of economic theory. This labour market was not working well. Maybe in time this market inefficiency would have cured itself. Maybe not. Perhaps it would have been better to take some action, rather than wait for a self-correction which may not have occurred. Even in this simple example there were a range of policy options, and it is far from clear what to do.

Fixing the wage of migrant labour by law is a possibility. Probably not a good one. Firms with the greatest need could not bid labour away from other firms in the normal way. The temptation to cheat would be great. Letting workers off early and other forms of cheating would promote an anti-social culture. A fixed wage regime would be very difficult to enforce.

As the cause of the problem is misinformation, an approach through information might be best. Who are the migrant workers? It is summer work. Maybe they are largely university students. With a limited budget, word could be spread that last year's high pay is unlikely to be repeated. If the message is effective, the ensuing pay will be higher than the normal slump. If the messaging is very effective, it could cause a high wage season by very few workers making the journey.

But what if the information is not believed? People might feel they were being tricked to stay away from high wages in Alaska and go in even larger numbers. Cautious policy moves have to allow for misjudgements of responses.

A further option would be to require work permits. These could be lowered or raised to control the flow of migrant labour. This is an uncertain tool. Greater certainty could be achieved by issuing a fixed number of permits. The benefit would go to workers who were saved from making a disappointing journey. But what about the Alaskan employers? Would they support a policy that potentially stabilised wages, or would they prefer to stick with the cycle of fluctuating wages with the occasional low wage year? It depends on how many permits were issued. For the scheme to be effective, the number of permits has to be such as to all being taken up every year.

The example illustrates the point that policy interventions have to predict responses reasonably accurately. In addition, careful attention must be given to who benefits and who loses.

4   Theories and Models

These notions of supply and demand and competition play a big role in economics. To get a better look at these propositions we need, among other things, to understand the distinction between theories and models. This is important, but not easy. A whole fringe intellectual industry has sprung up on nothing more than a misunderstanding of models and their place in economics. Here in a nutshell is a better understanding of theories and models.

Theories are broad explanations in general terms. Prices are determined by supply and demand is one such theory. It may be a pretty good explanation of some prices, but not so good for others. Suppose there is an attraction, say a natural cave, that people can visit. How much will the owner charge for visiting the cave? Let's assume he wants to collect as much revenue as he can from marketing the cave attraction. Let's also assume the number of visitors rises with a lower price, or equivalently, falls with a higher price.

A very low price may maximise the number of visitors. The owner's revenue is price per visitor times the number of visitors, so he sets the price at the level that maximises this relation. This analysis rests crucially on a model of the relation between price and quantity. Economists call that relationship a demand curve.

Making the relationship between price and the amount demanded explicit can be an improvement over simply holding that price is determined by supply and demand. If the government were to tax the cave owner, there are many possible means of doing this. One could tax per visitor or have an annual lump sum tax. The latter is easier to collect as it does not depend on accurate reporting about visitor numbers. But it will tax too much or too little, depending on the revenue of the attraction.

Governments should be concerned with the consequences of taxation and usually are concerned. How will the tax affect the level of consumption, the price charged, and so on? The answers to questions of this kind depend on having a model. The general view that the amount consumed is influenced by price will not suffice. In the example of the cave the model of the demand curve implies that the lump sum tax will not affect the price charged. The attraction owner will still set the price at the revenue maximising level. What about a specific tax on each ticket sold? A quick aside is needed here. We are assuming that the visitors respond to the total price including the tax. The attraction owner could advertise that his price has not changed and there now is a per ticket tax in addition to the price. It is conceivable that potential visitors would respond differently compared to a simple change in total price, but probably not.

What will the owner who wants to maximise his after-tax income do in response to the tax? Will he raise his price including the tax? There are two forces at work here. A higher price will reduce total revenue. It will also pass some, or even all, of the tax burden on to the visitors depending on the total price level chosen. Which is better for the cave owner? A bit of mathematics will show that the gain from passing on some or even all of the tax to visitors will be more than offset by the loss in total revenue. So again, the demand curve model will show that the owner absorbs the tax and there is no change in price to the visitor.

This conclusion of no change in price depends on the assumption of no effect of cost on supply. The cost to the owner of providing the cave does not change whether there are a few or many visitors. The more general case where changes in supply do affect the cost of the operation requires a more elaborate model. Typically, a specific tax, that is a per unit of sale tax, will raise price, but by less than the amount of the tax. The mathematics is a bit more demanding to show this result. This taxation analysis can be applied to markets with many competing producers. Again, this increases the level of mathematics needed.

When we look at actual markets, the imposition of a specific tax often raises the price by the full amount of the tax, or even more. Why is this? Why does the model often fail to predict accurately and gives the wrong answer? A good starting point is to consider whether the decision takers in firms know the prevailing magnitudes of the demand they are facing? Forgetting about the tax for the moment, it could be that the market price is optimal. Lowering the price or raising the price will lower their profits. But maybe the price is a stab in the dark based more on guesswork and convention. What the firms do know is that at a point in time all their competitors will face the same specific tax. Managers do not know what others will do. They fear being blindsided by setting a price too high so losing market share, or too low and sacrificing income. By doing what they think others will do, they may hope to minimise the risk of criticism.

Another consideration is the reluctance of firms to change prices. Consumers can act badly to uncertainty, and there is always the danger of starting a price war in which all will lose out. But with the imposition of the tax prices will have to change. So why not anticipate future cost rises and make a substantial price increase now. And here we come to a big question. The model gave one answer, price rises by less than the tax. The additional considerations offer an explanation of why price might rise by the amount of the tax. Observations of what goes on in markets supports the additional considerations. So what is the point of the model?

The model provides essential structure to the analysis of potential market responses to taxation employing a simplified set of assumptions. The model directs attention to considerations that can influence the results. The reasoning about what is going on is clear and explicit in the model. To think that is the end of the story is a naïve use of the model. To proceed to thinking about the issue without a model is unlikely to home in on useful results.

Returning to the cave analysis, that unknown demand curve is postulated assuming nothing other than price changes. Maybe lowering the cave price will induce the owners of other attractions in the area to lower their prices, with losses all around. If the current price exists for a long time, consumers might resent a rise in price and stay away for some time. Perhaps a safer strategy would be to keep the current price and advertise a bit more.

Consider two conclusions from this discussion of the cave as an attraction. The first has to do with theories and models. The theory that prices are determined by supply and demand is a good theory in many cases, but it does not tell us much. An explicit mathematical model that describes the supply and demand relations tells us more.

In physics there is usually a single model associated with each theory. The theory becomes synonymous with the mathematical specification. In economics the theory, such as the theory of price, can be represented by any number of models. There may be a lagged response. The quantity of a product put on the market today may depend on the price last month. Demand and supply may respond a great deal to price changes or be very unresponsive over certain ranges. We have many possible models that can be instances of the theory.

The mention of advertising raises a challenging point. Producers and consumers react to changes in circumstances in many ways. They may hold inventories that can go up or down. Firms can advertise or modify the product. Price changes are likely to be a step into the unknown and may risk price wars. In times of inflation there is less reluctance to raise prices as competitors are also obliged to increase theirs. In times of general price stability, other means of adjusting to changes are often preferred.

Economic theory tends to overemphasise price adjustment compared to other adjustments. This is partly because it has a general application compared to the specifics of other adjustments. In addition, price is easier to incorporate in models than some changes such as product modification. Supply and demand may offer a good explanation of some prices but not of others. In the cave story the price is set by the monopoly cave owner and supply can meet any likely demand.

A particular model may be wrong even if the theory is correct. In the cave case, the model needs to specify something about the demand curve. Downward sloping is typically part of an economic model. Is it a straight line? This means that a given reduction in price, say 50 cents, results in, say, 200 more visitors whether we are moving from five dollars to 45 or from eight dollars to 75. If the response changes as we move along the demand curve, the relationship is non-linear.

For many practical issues, the degree of response to price changes is important. The quantity demanded if the price changes may change a lot or only change modestly. The policymaker will want to anticipate how much the demand for gin will fall if we impose a tax on gin. He may have a concern about the tax revenue and about the impact of the tax on the gin industry. Supply and demand is going on here, true enough. It is a relevant theory. For many applications, and in many cases to find out if this is the right theory, we need a model. A model is a more explicit statement than the general assertion of the theory. A theory can guide us in constructing a model and a model can reveal implications of a theory. A model may incorporate a small response to price changes or a large one, both on the part of consumers and producers.

We can take a break from asking how economists go about understanding economies, and warning! We are only at the foothills of a great mountain range, and ask instead what is the aim of the enterprise? What do economists want to learn about the economy? Anything about the economy could be the subject of investigation. There is an endless number of possibilities. Most of these are trivial and of no significance. There are surprises. What we thought was trivial may be important. But some enquiries are typical of economics as it has been practised over recent decades. A central concern is the working of the market.

5   Cost–Benefit Analysis

Common sense and firsthand knowledge can be helpful in making some decisions. This informal approach can be useless or worse in other situations. The decision to adopt or reject large-scale infrastructure projects for example calls for serious cost–benefit analysis. This economics investigation involves far more than simply adding up long lists of costs of the project proposal and long lists of benefits. Both the costs and the benefits interact with each other and with the wider economy in complex ways.

The price charged to consumers of the project is not a given amount and will determine the extent of use as well as the revenue generated. With a large project there are bound to be significant impacts on other aspects of the economy. The project may complement or reinforce other activities or may be in direct competition with some activities. Careful analysis is needed to identify and quantify the likely impacts. In many cases reliable estimates of their effects are elusive. The analysis can proceed by considering a broad range of relations and seeing how sensitive the results are to alternative assumptions of size and direction of impacts.

The values estimated for many possible benefits will depend on theoretical investigation. What values should be attached to a better consumer experience, timed saved and reduced congestion? These are not directly observable or simple matters. Various techniques can be employed resting on alternative assumptions to generate ballpark figures.

The costs as well as the benefits are not straightforward. Prices of inputs to the project will be affixed by adopting the project. Complex estimates and sensitivity analysis are required. Both the costs and the benefits will be spread over time, possibly quite long periods of time. Taking account of these elements of timing is important in determining the viability or otherwise of the proposed project.

With a large-scale endeavour there are likely winners and losers because of adopting the project. Some attempt of identifying the makeup and size of the various groups can be undertaken. Compensating the losers may be impractical or even impossible to do. However, a theoretical investigation of likely magnitudes can be undertaken, and this could influence the decision to go ahead with the project. The various considerations outlined in coming to a thoughtful and beneficial decision all rest heavily on an appreciation of the complex economic considerations which are involved.

It could be argued, and has been argued by economists, that if investment decisions were dependent on careful explicit investigation nothing would be undertaken. This is not an entirely foolish position. It is particularly applicable to private investment where the investor bears the cost if the project fails. When it comes to public projects, the decision-maker does not bear the cost. It is the taxpayer. I believe this strengthens the case for caution and thorough analysis. Several commentators have noted the tendency of government decision takers to favour large-scale projects over possibly more beneficial groups of smaller projects. No doubt ego and aggrandisement play a role. A committee can decide how many airplanes to buy. It takes a lot of knowledge and hard work to decides how many and what kind of spare parts to buy. The bias towards the grand rather than the detailed project can be seen everywhere.

Cost–benefit analysis, however imperfect, is the best safeguard. The too familiar cases of cost overrun have much to do with uninformed and lazy decision-makers who do not bear the costs.

6   Markets

Economists are naturally concerned about the workings and behaviour of markets, as markets are the major institution for production and consumption in virtually all countries. One way of putting the market question is to ask what will happen if we do nothing? This must be qualified by allowing for what we do normally, like providing a legal system to enforce contracts and discouraging child labour. In general, the market organises itself. Are there areas where the market fails to function properly? And what do we mean by "properly"? There is a lot of obvious pathology in markets such as unemployment, inflation, financial crises, and more. Are these events caused by something we do, or something we failed to do? Much research is directed to finding answers to this question.

Even if things are going well, to put it crudely, we still may want to act on the market. An obvious example is taxation of various kinds. We might tax income, or profits or property to support activities we do not want to leave to the market, like national defence and primary education.

In popular and governmental discussion, the whole issue of what to leave to the market and what should be done otherwise is bedevilled by ideology. Many believe that as much as possible should be done by the market as competition promotes efficiency and innovation. Others believe equally strongly that the profit motive can compromise other considerations, such as safety and fairness. Economics does not provide off-the-shelf answers to these questions. It does provide methods for impartial investigation. These include theories of how the economy works and methods for discerning the relevant facts.

Our little tale of how a cave owner might price entry to his attraction implicitly assumed that other attractions would not change their prices as the price of cave entry changed. This is called partial equilibrium analysis. It may be a reasonable approximation of how things work, but in some situations other producers may respond to competitors' price changes. Taking account of these kinds of interactions is called general equilibrium analysis. The mathematics involved can be formidable.

The ultimate example of the distinction between a theory and a model comes from analysis of markets. Adam Smith, the great Scottish philosopher, suggested that the wealth of a nation is not measured most appropriately by the amount of gold in its treasury, but rather by its ability to meet the consumption goals of its citizens. He further suggested that producers and consumers respond to prices in a free market, and this brings about an allocation of production which is responsive to consumer preferences. This is a powerful theory of great generality and with important implications. Smith also suggested important qualifications to his description of the achievements of the market. This qualification involves businessmen colluding together at the expense of consumers. This warning is commonly ignored by zealous advocates of the magic of the market.

7   Mathematical Depictions of the Market

Later economists with a mathematical predilection struggled to express Smith's theory of markets as a model. It is not easy. A simpler first pass is to assume there is a fixed amount of production of each product in the economy, and then derive a set of prices which, in the light of consumer preferences, will cause the market to clear. By clearing we mean that supply, now assumed fixed, is equal to demand for every product. There is no unsold product and no unfulfilled demand at the prevailing prices. We have Smith's verbal discussion of the workings of the market. What is the point of this precise and explicit model?

I once put that question, as politely as I could, to the leading figure in this research programme. He said that solving one mathematical problem revealed the next problem to be solved. This is an example of an internally driven research effort, in contrast to one driven by searching for a policy response to an economic problem or one addressing something strange and not understood.

One objective of mathematical model building in economics is to establish a kind of existence argument. Smith said that the hidden hand of responses to price will direct an economy to function in a helpful way. The economy can be observed to work, but is it doing reasonably well? The verbal argument does not tell us much, one way or the other. The formal mathematical model can, at least for this highly simplified example, suggest that such a self-regulating system might function as Smith suggested. Had it not been possible to write down such a model, or at least none was found, the hidden hand argument might be in some doubt.

More complicated general equilibrium models of a self-regulating market economy have been constructed. Some allow for the volume of production of individual items to respond to price signals. These models include overall limits on the amount of labour and capital in the economy. The assumption here is that for every activity labour and capital combine, in specific combinations, to produce output. Other inputs, such as land and raw materials, are often not included in these models.

Beyond the mere suggestion of the possibility of a self-regulating economy, the model builders may manipulate their construction to answer questions like, is there one set of prices that will clear all the individual markets, or might there be more than one market clearing set of prices, and if so, how do they compare in terms of meeting the needs of the society? And then there are questions of stability. If the economy is disturbed in some way, will it tend to self-correct back to the equilibrium price configuration? Many other more subtle questions can be explored through the mathematical investigation.

Now we come to a big point, and maybe more than one. Are these investigations, difficult and demanding as they are, offering a good approximation to the workings of actual economies? Only the truly faithful, those who feel that self-regulating markets are something between natural, inevitable, and optimal, will take this general equilibrium story at face value, as literally true. Common sense says that if there is a large demand for a product, the price will rise, both choking off demand and increasing the incentive to produce more, and at some point, a price will emerge where everyone who is prepared to pay the price will get the amount they want, and no producer will be left with unsold stocks.

Common sense. If that is doing the job, why do we need the elaborate mathematical models? At this point we should register, for future reference, that other less ambitious models are commonly used in economics to great effect.

We have already given a partial answer about the point of models of the entire market. If we cannot show the possibility of a set of prices for our simple self-regulating model, can we have confidence in our understanding of actual economies? A more convincing and profound answer lies in the learning experience of the model builders and the 'feel', for lack of a better term, that they gain for exploring the functioning of self-regulating models. All economists get some exposure to this activity and hopefully some similar benefit.

8   Abstraction and Realism

Consider for a moment the question of how does the economy arrive at the market clearing set of prices? In many models, we simply solve the equations to arrive at the market clearing prices. Actual markets must go through a process, a trial-and-error learning process. Transactions occur at prices away from the market clearing prices. And this process never ends. New products are coming on the market and costs of production are changing. Is the notion of an equilibrium out there helpful in thinking about this ever-changing system? The answer is 'yes'. To explain how and why a structure of theory departing strongly from what it purports to understand can be of great use takes us to the heart of economic investigation. Considerable explanation and elaboration are needed.

Some economies in low-income countries with parts of the economy highly dispersed and isolated function very differently from markets in the digital world. Buyers and sellers meet infrequently on specified days and travel significant distances to do so. Failure to sell what was intended or to buy what was desired are both costly. When the market participants gather, an experienced trader looks over what has been brought and assesses the demand from customers and announces a set of prices. These prices are intended to be market clearing. Given the skill of the organiser, they usually are at least approximately market clearing. Trades do not take place away from the suggested clearing prices. This is an esoteric case of a market behaving much like some highly abstract economic theory. There are many examples where a partially realistic model turns out to be enlightening. An important part of the skill of a model builder is choosing assumptions that do not bias the results. These are what we might call innocent assumptions. They help to complete the model and may be very unrealistic.

9   Illegal Markets

A model intended to apply to a particular market, say the cocaine market in California, can suggest policy interventions. We need answers to questions like what will happen under various enforcement regimes. Typically, without some quantitative information about responses, we can only get qualitative answers. These are answers like the price went up or consumption fell. We do not know by how big or small these responses would be; we only gain insight into the direction of change, up or down, or not at all. It is limited information, but it can be useful nevertheless. More precise quantitative information depends on putting econometric meat on the model's skeleton. More on econometrics later.

The theory that the price of cocaine and the amount consumed in California are determined by supply and demand may well be a reasonably good theory. The theory does not help answer questions like what will happen if we apply various enforcement policies to this market. To get answers to policy questions we need a model. Here is a pretty simple one. Let's assume the drug is produced by farmers who will devote more agricultural resources, land and labour to cocaine if the price is higher. Being illegal, smuggling and distribution costs are high in addition to agricultural costs and raise the price to consumers by a fixed amount per unit sold.

On the demand side, let's assume the quantity purchased does not vary much, if at all, as the price goes up or down. At the extremes where price might be very low or very high, we would observe significant changes in demand. We are assuming that over a sort of middle range, the quantity purchased does not change much with price changes. Soon we will come to consider the issue of the accuracy of our assumptions but for now let's work with the model.

The drug dealers' revenue is the difference between what they pay the farmers and what they collect from users. Presumably a portion of this revenue is profits. Consider two different policy options. We can concentrate our enforcement efforts on the dealers, or we can go after consumers. If we attack dealers, the cost of dealing will go up. We will expect to see a higher price of cocaine in California. Dealer revenue will go up. What will happen to dealer profits is a little uncertain, but the quantity consumed will remain unchanged.

If we concentrate our efforts on consumers of cocaine, with arrests for purchasing and possession for personal use, some users will go to jail, and some will be frightened off using the drug. Demand will fall. Price will fall and so will dealer revenue. The model does not say so, yet, but dealer profits might fall as well. The model delivers clear answers. Attack dealers and the price will rise, and consumption will remain the same. Attack consumers and price will fall and so will consumption.

If this analysis is correct, it makes more sense to go after consumers rather than to concentrate enforcement activity on the drug dealers. With that policy, drug consumption goes down and so does dealer revenue. Isn't that what we want from our war on drugs? Yet in California and in most other places enforcement concentrates on dealers, which increases dealer revenue and has little or no effect on the use of cocaine. Why is the wrong policy commonly employed?

Perhaps legislators, enforcement agencies, and the general public are unaware of this economic analysis of the drug market. This may be a factor. Misunderstanding of simple economics is widespread. This section goes some way to explaining how intuition can give incorrect answers to economic questions. No doubt another factor is at work here, leading to what we might call the wrong policy emphasis. It is widely believed that something should be done about recreational use of drugs. Maybe some should be legalised, but what about the rest?

My guess is that the legislators and the drug users tend to come from the more affluent classes and the dealers from the poorer classes, not entirely, but somewhat. So it is socially less disruptive and easier to support the policy of attacking dealers, even if it makes little economic sense. Incidentally, this analysis of a drug market has surprising implications for the problem of global warming. We will come to that much later.

Hold on a moment. Isn't there something seriously wrong with our model of the California cocaine market? If demand does not go down much, or even at all with a price rise, why don't the dealers raise the price to the level where demand starts to go down prior to any enhanced enforcement? In earlier sections I discuss the interconnected nature of theory, including economic theory. Common assumptions about behaviour run across most aspects of economic theory. These include a preference for more profits over less profits. The cocaine market model appears to violate that assumption. That is a weakness, and it has to be addressed.

We could try some assumptions to get us out of this apparent inconsistency in the model. We want to base our analysis on the assumption that dealers prefer a larger revenue and profits to a smaller one. A possible way out might be to assume the California dealers are in competition with each other. Raising the price higher than the traditional price given the level of enforcement would lose market share, begging the question of how the 'traditional' price emerged. Alternatively, we could assume there is in effect a monopoly supplier with lots of little helpers. He sets a price that generates a healthy profit but does not attract outsiders to attempt to enter the market and start a drug dealer war.

These are possible strategies for rescuing our model. Let's try another tack and assume the price of cocaine in California is determined by an upward sloping supply curve, meaning at a higher price more cocaine is supplied, and a downward sloping demand curve, meaning that at a higher price less is purchased. Now what happens under different enforcement regimes?

Going after dealers raises the price and consumption falls. Going after consumers lowers the price and consumption falls. Given a primary concern with the amount of drug consumed and not about dealer revenue or profits, we see that consumption falls under both policies. How much it falls under each policy depends on the sizes of the responses of supply and demand after a given expenditure on enforcement. The model tells us where to look. It tells us what information we need to compare these policies effectively. The model alone does not answer the policy question.

10   Theories in Context

This is a really big and crucial aspect of economics as a means of gaining understanding. If you want to know how long it takes for light to get from a star a known distance away to the Earth, there is an off-the-shelf answer. Economics has few off-the-shelf answers. Is high speed rail a good idea for the United Kingdom? Do we need to raise interest rates now to avoid further damaging inflation? Should we use our limited policing resources to attack suppliers or consumers of illegal drugs? Will leaving the European Union benefit the United Kingdom economy in the long run, and how long is that? It would be great if we could go to the economics library and pull a volume off the shelf to give us these answers. We cannot, the shelf is almost empty. We have a large body of economic theory, a great bundle of economic explanations. What are they for? How do they contribute to economic understanding?

Economic theory structures our investigation of aspects of the economy. The theory alone rarely gives reliable answers to questions of policy. That does not mean theory is unimportant or useless. Absolutely not. Theory is vital. But more is needed. Why is that? Part of the explanation has to do with the concept of equilibrium. Take the policy of placing a tax on sugary drinks. A possible method of analysis is to assume that the drinks market is in equilibrium now and ask what the equilibrium after the tax will look like. This method makes a difficult measurement problem somewhat solvable. An alternative approach is to assume continuous adjustment over time. Now producers and consumers are reacting over time and the nature of those reactions is complex.

A related difficulty is changing responses on the part of consumers and suppliers. There is a tendency to rely on the law of large numbers. Each consumer is an individual with unique behaviours. Individual responses may cancel out, allowing us to predict the response of the consuming group as a whole. There are cases where this assumption of cancelling out may apply. More common are significant shared changes in group behaviour as a result of group experiences. Herd behaviour is common, but hard to anticipate. We can take a stab at postulating how consumers learn over time. Often the group confounds our expectations such as when consumers ignore the price increase brought about by the tax and assume others are doing the same.

11 One Set of Theories, Many Economies

Historically there has been some attempt to construct economic theories applicable to different kinds of economies. Some effort has been made to unravel the workings of planned or socialist economies. A larger effort concentrates on poor economies, sometimes called traditional economies, and more often designated as less developed economies. Some work persists along these lines. The bigger thrust is towards a more generally applicable theory.

Most economic theory is not about a particular economy, or even a particular kind of economy. Economies differ significantly, even between Western industrial market economies. Offering free vaccinations to give some protection against a virus will result in a large take-up in some countries. Another society may have a small take-up. In one society raising income tax may have little effect on how much people work. In another society to maintain the level of their after-tax income people may work more. Societies change over time, sometimes rapidly. A war or an explosive bout of inflation can alter behaviour. Economists are aware of these considerations. The various ways of dealing with unique and differing responses are central to economics methods and practices.

We have discussed the role of models as specific expressions of theory. Consider the amount of their income people save. Different levels of saving can have dramatically different effects on an economy. The amount of saving going on in a country depends on a variety of factors. Theory identifies factors such as income, wealth holding, and anticipated and unanticipated changes in income and wealth, along with widely held views about the state and prospects of the economy. The age structure of a country can influence behaviour with respect to how much people save. Explicit analysis of how these factors interact requires a model, a mathematical specification. One can get somewhere without a model, and we will look at the place of theory without models. For now, the issue is models.

A model involves assumptions. In the first model of the California cocaine market discussed above, a key assumption was that consumption did not respond to price changes. This led directly to the conclusion that concentrating enforcement on consumers was more effective than concentrating on dealers. This dependence on a certain assumption to drive the result is a weakness. A revealing analysis should not build the conclusion into the model. It should derive conclusion from the interactions of the model. Of course, if in fact consumers will not respond to price changes, or only insignificantly, that early model is very helpful. It informs the policymaker.

All models are abstractions from reality. Hopefully they give some insight into an aspect of the economy. Hopefully, what is left out of the analysis is less important. Many assumptions are employed because they simplify the investigation. There is always a danger that an apparently innocent simplification may distort the implications and mislead the investigator.

Less common today, but quite common in the past, was to assume that consumers were in full possession of all the information that was relevant to their decisions. More common today is to assume information is limited, imperfect, and costly to acquire and process. In the jargon this is called bounded rationality. Some markets may function poorly, or even fail to work at all, because some people have information that others lack.

The seller of a used car may know more about the car than a potential buyer. The seeker of health insurance may know more about his health than a potential insurer. For this reason, universal mandatory health insurance may do better than a freer health insurance market. To call the one socialism is ridiculous. It is an attempt to frighten people away from and to discourage thinking about alternatives. Assumptions about what people know and who knows what can play a critical role in some models and how we think about policy. In other situations they may be unimportant.

12   Realism of Assumptions

Economists have debated about the realism of assumptions in models. Some have held that if the model produces predictions in accord or in reasonable accord with the facts, that is all that matters. This is called an instrumentalist view of science. In my opening discussion I characterised science as seeking understanding. I slipped something by the unwary reader. What about the ability to control, to bring about results? Discovering a pill that relieves pain can be useful, even if we have no idea how it works.

I'm told by physicists that something called quantum electrodynamics is one of the most successful theories in physics. It makes extremely accurate predictions, and no one knows how it works. I take their word for this, knowing nothing about it. Some economists have argued similarly that the realism of assumptions in economics is of no importance. Getting the right predictions when we apply policy to an economy is what matters.

If economists had something approaching the degree of success of physicists in predicting the outcome of interventions, an instrumentalist approach could be of some use in some problems in economics. Lacking any such mechanical predictive success, I am opposed to instrumentalist approaches in economics. Others disagree with me for what I think are self-serving reasons. I will get on to that.

Competition is a major consideration in economics. Economists know more about competition than any other scientists, natural or social. Biologists have borrowed a lot from economics in explaining many things including aspects of the behaviour of wasps, fishes, birds, foxes, and many more. A wag once suggested that economics is about 'I'll do this for you if you do that for me'. Political science is about, 'I'll do this to you unless you do that for me'. And sociology is about, 'let's do this together'. Pinches of salt required, but no doubt economics emphasises and says a lot about competition.

Malicious interpreters claim that economics says competition is a good thing. Nonsense! Science, social or natural, can attempt to explain what is going on. Whether an outcome is good or bad depends on your values and possibly on what philosophers think about it. A good thing or a bad thing, competition plays a big role in economics, along with other considerations.

Traditionally economists used a four-way classification of competition in markets. Some markets were assumed to be perfectly competitive. The idea here was there were many buyers and sellers. No one could influence price. Everyone was a price taker. Prices were set by the market. If a seller tried to put his price up, no one would purchase from him. There was no reason to put his price down as being small in the market, he could sell all he could produce at the going price. Imperfect competition allows for some degree of producer control of price, due, for example, to brand image, though still subject to competition from rival products. Monopoly is the third category, with a single supplier. And oligopoly was the fourth kind of competition, with a small number of competitors. Market classification changed dramatically in later years, and I will get on to that analysis about strategic behaviour later in this chapter.

Assumptions about which type of market prevails are important in many investigations. Some economists have argued that one should always assume perfect competition, as this leads to correct predictions in response to policy moves. This claim is pernicious in several respects. Firstly, the claim regarding predictions is wrong. There is no large body of successful predictions. Secondly, it sweeps under the carpet the numerous outrageous violations of decent market practice. Third, it advances a spurious claim about the value of prediction over understanding what is going on. And finally, it supports an unwarranted faith in the market as the answer to all problems. More on a reasonable view of the market later.

The claim that realism does not matter has been used to promote a policy stance in favour of doing as much as is humanly possible through an unregulated market. I hope my arguments against this practice are persuasive. At the same time, we have to recognise that in order to get a handle on something as complex as an economy we need a model and that entails assumptions that simplify reality. Economists try to make their assumptions as innocent as possible with respect to biasing the results. An extreme error is to build models which in effect assume the result.

There is a careless tendency among many economists to reason as if there were some ideas which can appropriately be taken to be assumptions in all investigations. Wrong. Assumptions are what we take to be the case for a particular investigation. Other things are under investigation. For present purposes, we are taking some things to be the case. However, what is an assumption in one study might be under investigation in another study. In one study I might assume that an industry is working at close to full capacity as I examine the implications of a tariff. In another study I might be investigating precisely the degree of pressure on capacity in that industry.

All analysis is an abstraction from reality and a simplification. Part of the skill of an economic investigator is choosing assumptions that are manageable and close enough to reality to give answers which are reliable. Economists used to believe something called Gresham's law. The idea is that if two currencies are circulating in an economy at an official rate of exchange, and one is worth less than the official rate, people will always pay debts with the weak currency. Hence the phrase, bad money drives out good. Is this analysis correct?

One should always be on guard against propositions which depend solely on reasoning alone and have no need for evidence, for the facts. If everyone is aware that the official rate is one for one, but the true rate is two of the weak currency for one of the strong, people will be indifferent between being paid two of the weak or one of the strong. This is a beautiful little example of the challenge of doing economics. A plausible proposition turns out to be questionable, and even wrong, depending on the beliefs and information of the population. Further complications, such as a portion of the population holding accurate views about the currencies rather than everyone sharing the same views changes the bad money drives out good rule. Still more complication follows from the expectations people hold about possible inflation.

There is no iron rule about what we should assume about the nature of competition in markets, whether these are markets for currencies, services, or anything else. Assuming perfect competition may do little harm in one investigation. Another exercise may have the goal of finding out the prevailing mode of competition.

13 Strategic Behaviour

More recent developments called game theory have had a huge impact on economists' notions of competition and other aspects of economic life, such as what is rational behaviour? Incidentally, I would argue that game theory is not a good name for this branch of mathematics. The initiators thought this development might have something useful to say about poker, for example. So far it has turned out that is not the case. Game theory has turned out to be very useful in the analysis of situations where a small number of competitors, typically two, face each other, be it firms in competition, or butterflies seeking mates.

Incidentally, game theory, and several other branches of economic theory, have more straightforward success in explaining animal behaviour than with economic matters. I put this down to animals, and insects, having less complicated goals and being less inclined to change the way they behave.

A game theory analysis starts out by identifying the participants. Who are the players in this encounter? Next comes the choices open to all participants, and the consequences for them depending on what action they take and the other participants take. In most situations participants do not know what action competitors will take. In some situation a potential entrepreneur faces an array of competitors. He might open a pizza joint or a burger joint. The more burger outlets the better the returns to pizza places, and vice versa. Equilibrium occurs when the returns to both are equal at some mix of the two fast food outlets.

Consider pigeons competing for food. They can act aggressively by challenging other pigeons, or act passively waiting for non-challenging opportunities. If most pigeons are aggressive, the payoff to the passive strategy is higher, as costly fights are avoided. If most pigeons are passive, an aggressive strategy will yield more food, with few fights. An equilibrium occurs where the proportions of aggressive and passive participants are such that the payoffs to both strategies are equal. Numerous applications of strategic analysis have proved useful in economics and other settings.

A classic well-known game is called the prisoner's dilemma. Two individuals are suspected of a robbery. The police need a confession. The suspects are interviewed separately. They are faced with the following incentives. Claiming innocence when the other suspect confesses results in the maximum penalty. Confessing when the other suspect pleads innocence results in a small penalty. If both claim innocence, there is a small positive outcome for both. Neither suspect knows what the other will do. Confessing is the wiser strategy whatever the fellow suspect chooses to do. If his accomplice pleads innocence the reward is great. If the other suspect also confesses, the penalty of a confession is much less than pleading innocence.

What should a small country do with the threat of climate change? Undertake costly steps to reduce emissions, or do nothing and hope those steps are taken by other countries? If the other countries do, fine. Whether they do or not, it is in the small country's interests not to reduce emissions. A difficult problem of national incentives. However, there may be other considerations such as becoming a leader in alternative energy generation which could be of benefit to the economy of that small country.

14   Spatial Competition

Before turning to a sweeping overview of economics we can look at spatial competition. If there are two ice cream sellers on a beach, most customers will go to the nearest seller. If the two spread out along the beach reasonably far apart, they can minimise the distance customers will have to travel to buy ice cream. This is a socially admirable dispersion benefitting customers. But any seller can increase his share of sales by moving closer to the other seller. He loses no sales from the customers he is moving away from as he is still the closest vender. And by moving closer to the other seller he picks up some of that seller's potential customers. The two will wind up a short distance apart near the middle, not so good for convenient purchasing.

Economists have analysed similar central clustering. This can be seen over a great range of activities from policies of political parties to product features chosen by manufacturers. If your hammer is a bit heavier than any on the market, you will capture all the sales from those wanting a heavy hammer. Being more than a bit heavier may meet customer needs better, but market share increases from being only a bit heavier. It appears that competition can result in a sub-optimal allocation in space, broadly considered including product space as well as geographic space such as the location of petrol stations.

The competitive story gets more complex as more suppliers enter the market. With three suppliers, the worst position is to be boxed in the middle, with a supplier on both sides. To avoid being restricted to a small market share, supermarkets and computer manufacturers and many other activities might locate in a position where new entrants will do them little harm and not risk being boxed in, rather than where current sales are maximised. This is yet another example where a simple and quite plausible theory, namely a kind of market failure through central clustering, breaks down under additional plausible considerations.

In economic affairs it is rare for a theory to apply unreservedly or universally. Why is that? Two factors are especially important. The behaviour of the economy in response to policy interventions and other events, like an unusually cold winter, depends on what people do. A theory which says there are lots of different people out there and they behave in a great variety of ways may have some truth to it. It rather leads to the conclusion that we do not know what will happen. Secondly, past responses may give a poor indication of the coming response. Economists have tended to opt for choosing a few simple assumptions about reactions that will yield predictions.

15   Policy Consequences

Economists know that people are complex, idiosyncratic, and varied. As a result of this assumption, analytical strategies are usually adopted postulating that market participants, often designated as agents, have the goal of maximising something. Business firms are assumed to maximise profits. Fair enough, but complications abound. Is it profits in the short run or the long run? One might get more elaborate and suggest that firms strive to maximise the present value of a discounted stream of profits stretching far into the future. But can a firm ever know enough to adopt this goal as a practical working guide to action? Probably not.

The dominant strategy adopted by economists is to assume quite simple objectives on the part of agents. Typically, this involves relatively short-run pursuits of rather narrowly defined self-interest. In many cases this assumption is prompted by failsafe policy advice. It is safer to assume that some people will act dishonestly in their self-interest if there are no penalties for bad behaviour. If everyone behaves honestly, no harm is done by assuming otherwise. If in fact some people cheat, assuming otherwise is costly. Random checks may deter cheating. But this failsafe argument faces a problem. Assuming cheating may encourage cheating. The absence of random checks may promote a culture of honesty. It may not. It all depends on how people respond, the great challenge for economists.

16   Economics and the Just Society

A society where trust is the norm and most people believe others can be trusted is a good state of affairs. Not only is it efficient and saves on enforcement costs, but also people relate to each other in a more respectful and caring way. Economic arrangements have a bearing on how people relate to other people. Policy on income distribution and many other issues benefits from awareness of these side effects. An agreed sense of fairness and a concern for fairness benefit a society.

Profit maximising of some variety may be a plausible working assumption, but what about the giant firm and its million a year or more CEO's remuneration? His objectives might have more to do with keeping shareholders happy in the short run and increasing his take. Morality comes into the story.

Economists study illegal behaviour. Others might say it should be a problem for the legal system and leave it at that. Perhaps. Laws take time to enact and to enforce. Drafting is never perfect and complete. Armies of lawyers work to find ways to subvert the intentions of the legislators. The political process itself can bend to accommodate powerful wealthy interests. A pessimistic view holds that inequality has gone so far that reform is now impossible. Let's hope otherwise.

Economists do give attention to costs of enforcement and warn against policies and arrangements which reward breaking the rules. Minimising incentives to break the rules may be a preferred policy option compared to policies that require vigorous policing. Taxation may be an exception to this principle. It may take considerable effort to collect income taxes. This may be a preferred option to raising tax rates and lead to a more just society.

17   Specialisms in Economics

The economy is a vast area for investigation. As with any scientific enquiry, a complex array of specialisms has evolved to break down the economy into manageable chunks for investigation. The role of money and the management of the quantity of money is one of these. We will have more to say about money. Many innocent observers think that economics is about money and little else. This misunderstanding will be addressed.

It would make tedious reading to list the many specialists in economics, but it is interesting to think about the structure of specialisation in the subject. One way economists divide up the economy is by particular markets. We can draw on two of these for the purpose of illustration.

Participation in the labour market has a direct impact on most individuals and families. Is the wage determined by supply and demand for labour? Prestige and the power of managers in large firms may depend on the number of people in their units. Will the managers aim for a tight operation with maximum efficiency, or for trying to make themselves more important by expanding the size of their department? What about built-in labour surplus so the unit can operate effectively when people are off sick, or on maternity leave, or quit unexpectedly?

Paying a wage above the market clearing rate may reduce turnover costs. It may discourage the workers from stealing the tools. Labour economists explore a huge array of questions such as the impact of trade unions and the effects of minimum wages. They often observe outcomes that depart from what we might expect to see from straightforward competitive models. Minimum wage legislation may have little effect on employment, contrary to expectations. These and related puzzles call for further investigation.

Economists who are particularly enthusiastic about the market have suggested that competition will tend to eliminate discrimination. If for example women are paid less than the competitive wage, firms that employ more women will have an advantage and eventually eliminate discrimination against women. Again, the evidence does not support this competitive insight. Why not? What is going on here? This is a common issue in economics. A simple and straightforward explanation of some economic observation appears to fit the facts in some cases and not in others. Economic theory provides a structure for further investigation.

Another specialism studies the relationship between the home country, so to speak, and the outside world. Standard areas are international trade, migration, and capital movements. Indirect investment is when interests in one country buy shares or other assets in another country. Direct investment is when interests in one country, typically corporate interests, produce goods or services in another country. These sub-divisions of international economics can be broken down further.

A specialist, be it in international economics, labour economics, agricultural economics, the economics of the professions, or whatever, draws on shared elements of economic theory. These include views of market behaviour and the objectives and actions of individual agents. Common techniques are employed for reasoning from the behaviour of agents to the functioning of the economic system. The use of evidence to flesh out models and test the validity of theories is common to all specialists.

The specialist needs a great deal of knowledge of the institutions that are important to his specialism. These vary significantly from one country to another. The specialist also needs to know much of the huge research findings in each field. This is sometimes referred to as the literature of the subject. The labour economist is familiar with labour legislation and trade union structure and much more. The international trade specialist in addition to the commonly held skills of enquiry knows tariff law and preferential trading blocks. Commodity groupings such as the International Coffee Agreement and OPEC are part of the field along with international institutions like the IMF, the World Bank, the World Trade Organization, and much more. And finally, all specialists have a good understanding of the broader economy in which their specialism is located.

Specialisms feed into each other. The labour market has multiple implications for investigations centred on the behaviour of firms. Foreign direct investment affects the labour market. Foreign owned firms often have different policies from domestic firms on labour management and trade unions. Migration can play an important role in sectors of the economy with a seasonal demand for labour and activities dependent on cheap labour. Some economists study the economy at large, but from a particular perspective. The focus is on the stability of the economy and the issues of inflation and unemployment.

18   Skilful Use of Theory

Economic theory is rarely successful on its own in explaining what is going on or informing economic policy. Why is that? Hints have been given throughout this chapter. What people believe about the future conditions and what makes sense to do today. Experience conditions what people believe, often in strange and mysterious ways. This is not a counsel of despair. Social science is not like natural science. There are things economists can do to respond to problems of theory on its own. We have mentioned some and will add more.

Economic theory is built around an emphasis on efficiency which helps in considering what to do. Efficiency is about achieving goals with limited resources. Many policy issues have important considerations with little to do with efficiency. Should we privatise prisons, water supply, and air traffic control? Again, this does not mean that economics cannot help with these and a myriad other policy issues. It does mean that the economics employed should be sensitive to considerations that go beyond efficiency.

The standard response that some economists make to this argument rests on the phrase cost/benefit analysis. The hope is that everything relevant to the decision can be given a monetary value. There is nothing silly or wrongheaded about this, if used with circumspection. For example, a privatised prison goes against the idea that only the state has the right to deny liberty. Is an agent of the state the same as the state acting? There is nothing in economics through assigning a monetary value that can answer that question.

A significant part of the skill of economists involves efforts to take some account of interactions and relationships between parts of the economy. Elements of the economy that may be relatively easy to understand on their own can lead to challenging complications when acting together. Technical change such as the development of the motor vehicle can bring about the decline of some sectors of the economy, but how will it affect income distribution, land values, and the general price level. Perhaps this is what a distinguished economist had in mind when he wrote that nothing in economics is both true and obvious other than the theory of comparative advantage, a core concept in international trade theory.

19   Comparative Advantage

It certainly is the case that the comparative advantage concept is not obvious. A distinguished professor of artificial intelligence said in a major lecture that humans have a comparative advantage over robots in certain areas. He should have said we have an absolute advantage or simply have an advantage. Comparative advantage is something else, as we shall see in some detail. Carefully working through this idea is revealing of several aspects of economics method.

We begin with the obvious point that an economy can produce different mixes, or combinations of goods. It seems that for a significant period of history, the Soviet Union had something of a surplus of radios and a severe shortage of television sets. Why was this situation allowed to persist? It would seem to make sense to move some resources, labour, materials, factory space, from radio manufacture to television sets. No doubt other adjustments were needed as well. It seems that no such reallocation took place, for reasons we need not go into now.

In any economy it is possible to reduce the production of some things in order to produce more of other things. For the purposes of explaining comparative advantage, I will assume we are dealing with two products made with one factor of production, possibly labour. Right away one could say, this is ridiculous. There are many products, tens of thousands, and many factors of production. What is the point of an idea that only applies to an absurd abstraction? Granted. But it can be shown that the idea put forward here can be generalised to many products and many factors of production. All that is needed is a bit of mathematics, which I will spare the reader.

The next simplification I will use, which also can be generalised, is that the rate of transformation of one product into another is constant. Let's say that in a day's work we can catch one deer or ten rabbits. This ratio remains constant whether we are catching mainly deer or mainly rabbits. The comparative advantage argument works equally well with a changing rate of transformation from one product to another. Let's drop deer and rabbits and call the products 'A' and 'B'. This rate of transformation quantifies the move from more A to less B, or the other way around. It is key to the comparative advantage concept.

Next, let's assume two countries. Again, no worries, we can make the same argument with any number of countries. Now assume both countries make A and B. Suppose the rate of transformation of A into B is the same in both countries. Now no mutually advantageous trade can take place between our two countries. The relative price of A and B is the same in both countries.

Turning now to the money price in the two countries. We can see that this depends on the exchange rate between the currencies. One possibility is that the rate is such that A and B cost the same in both countries. Now no trade takes place. If the relative price of A and B is the same in both countries, when the exchange rate is such that one product is cheaper, both products are cheaper. Again, no trade. Of course, one country could import both goods and borrow to pay for them. But let's confine our view of trade to mean exporting one thing and importing another.

So, there you have it. Profitable exporting does not depend on being able to produce the product less expensively than the other country. It depends on the relative price in one country compared to the relative prices in the other country. What we compare is relative prices, which reflect relative transformations, how much of one product we have to forgo in order to produce more of another.

A student once came up to me after a lecture and said in my country we used to buy where it was cheapest and sell where we could get the best price. But now I know we should trade according to comparative advantage. Of course, responding to prices is trading according to comparative advantage, at least in some cases.

Comparative advantage can be regarded as a possibility theorem, a statement that something is possible. In the case that something is mutually advantageous trade is possible between two countries, one of which is better at producing all products. And how much trade is like this? If one country exports oil to another with no oil that is an absolute advantage. At the present time, a dozen countries sell cars to each other and buy cars from each other. This has more to do with branding, small differences, and creating a unique product.

20   Money

Enough on international economics for the moment. Up to now we have ignored money in our discussion of economics. This is not an oversight. The economy produces food, clothing, housing, and legal services, among many other things. Money facilitates this activity, how things get produced and who gets what. Money is not the point, or an objective of the economy. No doubt some people want to acquire money for its own sake, not for what they may do with it. These are not the truly rich, the billionaires.

They hold a very small proportion of their wealth in money. Indeed, some billionaires may have negative money holding and do some borrowing. Their wealth is in the form of property, ownership of productive assets like shares in large corporations, and in racehorses and art objects. In times of inflation, where the value of money is declining, holding less money and more houses is a good idea.

A substantial body of economic theory deals with controlling inflation, or put another way, preserving the value of the currency. Interestingly, there is no unique measure of inflation. If prices generally are going up, but the prices a particular individual faces are not rising, for that individual inflation is zero. The combination of goods and their proportions as a measure of inflation depends on the consumption patterns of individual sectors of society. For many practical purposes we consider a broad range of consumption and construct an inflation measure for the economy as a whole.

A money economy is vastly more efficient than one based on barter. It is up to the monetary authorities of a country to attempt to secure the optimum amount of money for the economy. They have to take account of complex relations between such diverse matters as the cost of borrowing, incentives to investment and saving, the exchange rate between the home currency and other currencies, the stability of the banking system, and other considerations. Many countries opt for having these matters addressed by an independent central bank. Political parties in power may wish to see a temporary boom in the economy around election time regardless of longer-term consequences. This is part of the case for central bank independence.

Banks and investment markets are key players in the money system. They facilitate financing investment and affect the quantity of money in the system. Commercial banks cannot lend money they do not have. They do affect the quantity of money in the system as most of money lent returns to the banks and can be lent again. Regulation of the proportion of money held back and not lent is an important tool of the monetary authorities.

Banks borrow short-term through deposits. They lend long term in the form of mortgages and other loans. This is an inherently fragile arrangement. Depositors can ask for their money back at any time. Central banks stand by to back up commercial banks when they come under pressure. They also regulate the banks in terms of their asset holdings and lending practices. This is a complex balancing act of economic policy. Banking and finance are areas of intense specialist investigation, but all economists have working knowledge of these institutions as they influence all aspects of the economy.

Business firms usually limit borrowing from banks and instead seek investors through selling bonds, instruments with a fixed rate of return, or shares in the company. Finance experts study optimum combinations of financing. Once issued, shares go on being traded in what can look like a glorified casino. Authorities attempt to stabilise these markets, not always successfully. A justification for stock market trading is that investors would be reluctant to invest if they could not buy and sell their investments easily.

The consequences of smaller stock market bubbles and crashes are largely a matter for investors. Major political events impinge on the economy generally. A wave of bankruptcy and declining investment in new capacity by firms can lead to tragic levels of unemployment. Monetary authorities do what they can to dampen excessive reactions, partly by controlling the cost of borrowing. Major military conflicts can have similar consequences.

Achieving a more successful management of the monetary system of a country is neither simple nor purely mechanical. A thorough grasp of the theory linking aspects of the economy is essential for effective macro management. Once again, on its own this is not enough. For example, judgements must be made about how investors will respond. Like they did in the past or differently? Econometric analysis can help with these estimates, along with immersion in the workings of the economy.

21   Econometrics

Econometrics is about quantities and causal relations. Quantities are important. How much revenue will a tax rate change generate? What effect will an interest rate change have on investment? How will a change in the exchange rate affect inflation? How much will additional government expenditure affect unemployment? What will be the consequences of an increase in public debt?

Often theory can indicate the direction of change, up or down. Public policy usually depends on how much, as well as the direction. Raw data is needed for deriving various causal relationships in the economy. Very little data are collected for the purposes of economists. Most data are collected for other purposes and have to be manipulated and interpreted to be useful for economic analysis. This is highly specialised work but applied economists must have a good working knowledge of how data is generated, including changes in data collection over time.

Sophisticated statistical manipulation is needed to uncover genuine causal effects of one thing on another, say, interest rates on investment. Medical researchers have found a relationship between poor oral hygiene and heart disease. But maybe, on balance, people with fewer heart problems have better diets as well as better oral hygiene. Economists note that wages go up more when profits are high. And profits tend to be high in boom times when unemployment is low. What is causing what?

Advanced statistical investigation, usually called econometrics, employs diverse means to uncover underlying relationships. All aspects of the economy are buffeted about by political events, natural changes, some regular effects like seasonal swings, and some more idiosyncratic factors. In a continually changing world these 'noise' factors can obscure the causal relations. But there are no guarantees that there is a stable relationship to be uncovered.

The ratio of male to female babies born worldwide is quite stable, as you might expect. But after major wars the proportion of male births rises slightly. What is this about? It appears that stress levels have something to do with the birth ratio, or is this a reporting phenomenon?

Econometricians faced similar problems, but with less reason to think there is an unchanging relationship to be uncovered. In addition, data issues abound in economic enquiry. For example, it can be unclear if someone not working would prefer to be employed or perhaps no longer wants to work. Hence the difficulty of measuring unemployment.

Statistical techniques become more powerful with more data. Weekly figures may be better than monthly figures, and monthly figures better than quarterly data. But extra observations from shorter time intervals can contain less information for many enquiries. Longer runs of data involve the problem of underlying changes in the structure being studied. Brilliant work is done by econometricians, but there are limits to what can be achieved.

Economic policy advisers on interest rate decisions, for example, draw on economic theory, available evidence, and econometric analysis. The process of coming to a conclusion is not mechanical. It is not a matter of simply drawing on information and applying techniques. Why not? There are several reasons. There is uncertainty due to data inadequacies, current shocks to the economy, and possible future events. Different policies concentrate uncertainty in different ways. And even without uncertainty, policies benefit some interests and impose costs on others. There is no way of purely scientifically resolving these issues.

This does not mean that all is lost, or that one opinion is as good as another. Far from it. Social scientists in general, and economists in particular, have ways of gaining understanding in social situations. We will say more about these aspects of economic investigation.

22   Representative Studies

We have discussed evidence and the importance of facts but have not given many examples. Many tight and rigorous investigations have been undertaken in economics. These tend to be directed to relatively narrow past events rather than proposing new policies. They are much less prone to some of the complexities discussed above. They provide useful and quite reliable information about past events. In many cases these findings are likely to hold true into the future, but of course there are no guarantees.

Three fairly recent studies chosen more or less at random illustrate the case study aspect of economists at work. One study involves a puzzle that has troubled some economists. Not many observers outside of economics would share their concern. Data suggests that much criminal activity of young men is self-defeating. Careful accounting implies that the loss of earning power from having a criminal conviction outweighs the returns to crime. Why do these men behave so irrationally? The investigator in this case found what appeared to be a mistake in the use of data in previous studies where the critical assumption had been that the earnings potential of those committing crime was the same as those not committing crime. Clever data handling revealed that the criminals had a lower potential for earning legitimately than those not committing crime. So for the criminal group crime was a rational decision based on maximising income.

This conclusion appeals to economists who are prone to assuming that narrowly defined rationality goes a long way towards accounting for human behaviour. An alternative view would be ideas like they turned to crime because they fell in with the wrong crowd. But maybe 'the wrong crowd' is simply the path to a criminal career. This debate between those who explain behaviour on rational optimising grounds and those drawing on more mixed and socially determined explanations runs through much of social science including economics. Better policies regarding crime can depend on where the balance of truth lies.

A related study addresses reluctance on the part of many people to install solar panels. Some policymakers believe that solar panels are a good investment for the consumer, and the reluctance is due to habit, lack of information, and the like. The policymaker believes that subsidies that will nudge consumers to take the plunge are a good answer to this failure to act. The study finds otherwise. Solar panels are not a good investment for many potential consumers. Their reluctance to act is based on rational decision-making. A better policy would be to encourage research and other means such as no tariff on imports that could lower the cost of solar panels. Once again, the economists' usual preferred assumption of rational self-interest appears to be borne out. Now with rising electricity prices the incentives could change.

Some years ago, the United Kingdom took the unusual step of privatising air traffic control. This was done under a Labour government. The stated motive was that air traffic control required a considerable capital investment which should be borne by the air travellers, not by the general taxpayer. This is a good argument, though there are other ways of achieving that end other than privatising.

There was considerable interest in this decision in the United States. Advocates pro and con lined up with predictable arguments. Some said that privatising air traffic control would lead to more efficiency and innovation. Others maintained that privatising would put profits ahead of safety. With 10 years of history of a privatised air traffic control it was possible to investigate the results based on facts rather than ideology. The results were no change in 'near misses', as potential accidents are called, or other measures of safety. Greater attempts to promote United Kingdom techniques abroad did not emerge. Costs remained the same, apart from the remuneration of the most senior executives which rose considerably.

These three studies are illustrative of thousands undertaken by economists. They are relatively small scale addressing circumscribed issues. They combine theory with factual evidence, producing convincing results. The majority of studies of this kind produce findings of potential use to policymakers. Will they apply to other countries or the same countries in later years? Here is the rub. Unlike findings in physics, the social world is changing. The scale of operations changes. Technical change, new inventions, and so on change markets and non-market operations. Above all, what people believe and how they respond depends on experience and other influences. With uncertainty about the future, people make rational and irrational choices. Herd responses are common. Being unsure what to do, often people follow what others are doing.

These potential disruptions of economic expectations are less of a problem with more narrowly defined issues and over short periods of time. Economics works best in business-as-usual situations. Even here, without trained investigation, costly mistakes can be made. The drive for high-speed rail in the United Kingdom, against all disinterested and professional economic studies, is a powerful example. This is large scale. Many policy issues are also large scale. What one might think are simple matters, like interest rate changes, have reverberations throughout the economy. Joining or leaving an economic union or a shared currency are clearly large scale and far from business-as-usual decisions. How does economics work here?

23   Investigation and Immersion

A small digression will set the stage for addressing this key question for economists, how to proceed with ill-defined investigations. Two senior economics professors, one at the University of Chicago and one at the London School of Economics, employed a similar method of forecasting. There may be others. They forecast a whole variety of economic factors such as the change in total output in the economy, the rate of inflation, the level of unemployment, the size of public debt, the level of exports, and so on. They both were outstandingly accurate in their forecasts. They easily outperformed trend extrapolation, meaning the future will be a continuation of the past, and did better than the most sophisticated econometric forecasting. How did they do this?

In addition to the economic theory in each area, these professors immersed themselves in the questions under investigation. They read all relevant reports and speculations. They pored over the published statistics in the target area and related areas. Numerous interviews were conducted with businesspeople, trade unionists, government officials, journalists, and others. Then they ruminated and came out with forecasts. When asked about their methods, they could only describe what they did, not how the information collected led to the forecasts.

Is this simply common sense writ large? The answer is a firm 'no'. Two considerations are crucial. The first is a strong knowledge of the relevant theory. The second is a broad knowledge of the economy. My guess is if the American tried the same exercise in the United Kingdom, and vice versa in the United States, neither would do very well initially, but would improve over time. Theory is the key. The basic ability to reason in terms of who the participants are, what choices they have, what their motives or objectives are, and how these elements combine to produce an economy wide outcome is fundamental to economic enquiry. Equally important, in many cases, is the ability to employ theory sensitively and not mechanically.

24 Well-Defined and Ill-Defined Problems

Many economic issues and investigations are ill-defined in two very different ways. One has to do with sheer complexity. The physicist has a good theory of the movements of the planets, but not why there are nine of them, if that is the current agreed count. In principle if we knew how much material was out there around the sun and how it was distributed, we could explain the complex dynamic process that led to the nine planets. In fact, the complexity is overwhelming, and we can only wave our hands and suggest what happened. For many problems in economics the sheer complexity is so great that we can reason about broad underlying factors, but the investigations of our two professors are needed as well.

The second factor leading to economic problems being ill-defined is uncertainty about objectives. A larger total output is often taken to be a good thing, a worthy objective. Is a little less today to achieve more output in the future a good choice? A fable can be suggested as to how to arrive at the best growth path over time. Ultimately, the answer is blowing in the wind. And what about the environment. We will have more to say about nature and economic growth. In the United Kingdom there is talk about levelling up the economy. Would it be better if everyone went up by 10%, or the worst off went up by 15%?

A sensible answer is these questions are not issues for economists to decide. Social science, like natural science, can explain, or attempt to explain, what is going on, how things work, what causes what, and what will happen if you apply a certain policy. In many cases there can be guidance from the government or the culture of the society. But in many cases the issues are too complex and require too much understanding of the economy for clear and unambiguous objectives to emerge from anywhere.

25   Economies and Economic Advising

The task of the economic adviser is different from that of the two forecasting professors. They are saying what will be the average price of food next year. The adviser needs this kind of information, but something more in addition. He has to predict the consequences of policy interventions of various kinds. Economic theory, an understanding of how the economy works, plays a bigger role in policy interventions than in pure forecasting.

This does not mean that theory can be applied literally and mechanically without sophistication, scepticism, and caution. A few economists seem to think that we have a theory of how a self-regulating market works, and the actual market is just like that. More likely this is not merely a misuse of economics. Rather, it is an apology for the *status quo*. It is a drastic mistake to argue that if you do not have overwhelming evidence to the contrary, leave it to the unregulated market. Nothing in the social science economics justifies such a position.

Pure theory is vital. Factual knowledge is equally important. Uncritical advocates of the market tend to ignore market imperfections. Dealing with imperfections is a complex matter. An important theory known as the theory of the second best shows that in an economy with many imperfections, removing or reducing one imperfection may do harm rather than good. Once again, the successful application of theory requires factual knowledge.

This guided tour shows the heavy emphasis economists have placed on analysis of markets. This is appropriate. They are important and complex institutions. When conditions appear to demand it, governments step in to cap prices and amend the workings of the market in other ways. Setting the ground rules to promote efficiency and an appropriate level of investment, as well as a reasonable return to investors, is a challenge to economists, and much good work has been done along these lines.

Patent law is another area where economists have made important contributions. What should be subject to patents, and for how long, to encourage the search for innovation without granting excessive monopoly earnings? One activity, little practised these days, is to postulate a comprehensive planning regime, or a planned economy, that directs the economy to work like an ideal market. This work went on before the age of computers and referred to computational limitations. Even with computers the task is too difficult, not to mention the unappealing practice of directing labour to particular activities.

Economists have provided insights into less ambitious and comprehensive examples of planning, such as setting production targets for producing Spitfire planes in the Second World War. With good advice planners can do a reasonable job of deciding on the number of planes. Deciding on the number of spare parts to order among the 10,000 candidates is another matter. Planners can get their heads around a big project like high-speed rail in the United Kingdom. This, along with sheer political aggrandisement, has a lot to do with the rejection of the advice of economists to take a more detailed approach to rail investment.

This chapter is too long, and not nearly long enough. Economics is a huge undertaking. Over three centuries emphasis has moved from worry about what value is to understanding how the economy works and how it might work. Apologies to economists whose area of specialisation has been ignored. There are many of these. Economics has been defined as the study of the application of scarce resources to alternative ends. There is something in this, but the same applies to the problem of a football team. Economics is about the economy. It is about efficiency, but much more. What is needed to be an economist? The best answer came from Keynes.

He was troubled by the fact economics is not obviously such a demanding subject. Compared to the highest reaches of mathematics, physics, and the like, economics seems to be a less demanding undertaking. At the same time, Keynes feels that very few people do economics well. Why is that? His answer emphasises the variety of skills economists need.

> The master-economist must possess a rare combination of gifts.... He must be mathematician, historian, statesman, philosopher—in some degree. He must understand symbols and speak in words. He must contemplate the particular, in terms of the general, and touch abstract and concrete in the same flight of thought. He must study the present in the light of the past for the purposes of the future. No part of man's nature or his institutions must be entirely outside his regard. He must be purposeful and disinterested in a simultaneous mood, as aloof and incorruptible as an artist, yet sometimes as near to earth as a politician.

For me the key element is not so much the range of skills required. It is the great challenge of contemplating the particular in terms of the general, or as I would put it, employing theory along with modifying facts. And then comes that great phrase, touching abstract and concrete in the same flight of thought. Keynes published a paper in which he disparaged the use of econometric estimation of elements that figured prominently in his analysis of the macro economy. These included the consumption function, how consumption relates to income, and how investment responds to the interest rate. Why did Keynes object? My answer is that he feared that economists might employ his ideas as being sufficient in themselves without considering particular contexts. I think he feared that econometric findings would displace intuition and the flight of thought.

Perhaps Keynes worried a little too much. He rightly recognised that most economic issues are to some degree ill-defined. Treating them as if they were well-defined can lead to bad policy. But that need not be the case. The use of econometrics can complement a broader based investigation rather than being a substitute for it. There are balanced and competent advisers out there. It is a challenge to selectors to identify them.

6

Excessive Inequality

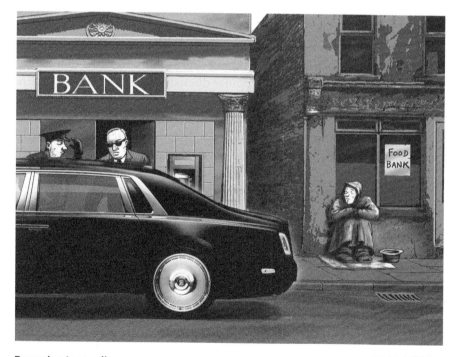

Excessive Inequality

This topic is not included in the economics chapter partly because we lack a crucial element in the theory of wealth inequality. How wealth inequality changes over time and differs across countries is a missing theory. Wealth inequality is an important topic calling for a separate chapter. I begin by addressing some flawed arguments.

It is wrong to claim that if you cannot specify the appropriate level of inequality, you cannot argue that current levels are excessive and that they have adverse consequences. Researching the consequences does not depend on specifying the appropriate level. As a scientific matter, consequences are just consequences. The notion of adverse effects brings something in addition to the discussion. Fair enough. But economic knowledge is a powerful engine for the promotion of better policies as determined by the culture of the society. Part of the job of the economist is to improve our understanding of the causes and consequences of inequality. Addressing these mistaken arguments is beating a dead horse, though it serves as an introduction to more serious considerations.

Economic inequality takes many forms. These include inequality of wealth or the net worth of individuals. It is important to think in terms of individuals, not the wealth of companies. Popular discussion tends to concentrate on giant firms and their tax avoiding strategies. The truly wealthy are delighted to see governments directing their attention and limited amounts of energy and resources to chasing business companies. Meanwhile, the excessive wealth of individuals is largely ignored. I will attempt to defend my use of the term 'excessive' shortly.

There is a pragmatic case for taxing profits on the argument that governments have to try to raise revenue however they can. And there is an economic case for companies to meet the costs of their activities such as dependence on infrastructure and the legal structure of a society. However, the extent of the use of these elements is not related to profits. The pragmatic case for taxing profits might take the line that while it makes more sense to tax individuals when they received income from ownership of companies, we often cannot do that effectively, so we might as well go for profits as a second best. There is also the consideration that income receiving individuals may be living in a foreign tax authority, so taxing profits generated at home is the only option. True enough. But wealth inequality is a global problem, and the primary focus should be on wealthy individuals.

Inequality of income comes from earnings in employment and returns to wealth holding such as dividends on shares. Some decades ago, the heads of large corporations in the United States and the United Kingdom earned on the order of 30 times the average wage in their companies. Now it is not uncommon for CEOs to earn 300 times the average of those they employ. Another aspect is the issue of inequality of opportunity. These inequality aspects are related and interact with each other. Giant CEO salaries can lead to dynasties of wealth holders whose only occupation is employing wealth managers. Inequality of opportunity can prevent investment in education and in undertaking entrepreneurial activity.

Here I am focusing on the most damaging type of inequality. In many countries about 1% of the population holds half the wealth or more of the entire country. Where we can observe the wealth holding of the top one-tenth of 1% the extremes are even more striking. A small number of economists, a very small number, have expressed the view that wealth inequality is of no concern to economic analysis. One can only speculate on the reasoning behind this mistaken view.

If inequality were exclusively a matter of morality or fairness, it might be left to philosophers. But even that narrow argument is flawed. We can attempt to explain differences in equality over time and place without passing judgement on it. Is that a potential matter for economic understanding? Some say 'yes' but add that they are not interested. Theirs is a personal statement, not a view about the proper scope of the discipline of economics.

As a personal preference it is strange, to say the least, to ignore inequality. In the United Kingdom today many public workers nurses, teachers, and others are on strike or contemplating strike action. Declining real income and resentment of senior executive salaries are legitimate motives. Government revenues can afford a tiny increase in pay for many in the public sector, or a substantial increase for one selected sector. But striking can only affect the push and shove between sectors, or possibly an inflationary increase for all. It does not affect the root cause.

There is strong evidence that inequality influences decision-making. In many cases it leads to short-term decision-making. The amount and kind of both investment and consumption are heavily influenced by inequality extremes. Some billionaires use their wealth to discover a treatment for malaria and invest in charitable activities. More use some of their wealth to build a bigger yacht than their fellow wealth holders, or take a brief journey into space.

Thomas Piketty has had a great success with his book on capital in the current setting. He and his colleagues undertook and reported on a mammoth effort to measure wealth inequality over time and across many places. It would have been helpful to have discussion of where their finding differed from those of other researchers, if they existed, and which were the better measures. But you cannot have everything, and in many countries their investigations were the first to be undertaken. Their great achievement was drawing attention to an important social and economic problem.

Piketty and his colleagues make a strong case, rather more by implication than by formal argument, for a wealth tax. Income tax adjustment cannot address the issue. So far there is little evidence that governments are preparing to act. Like the climate issue, there is a good deal of moaning and groaning, and little action.

It is sometimes claimed that international cooperation is required to introduce a wealth tax. This is false. It is also claimed that this is a complex matter and requires careful investigation. This is correct. Even a few extremely wealthy individuals have voiced the need for a wealth tax. It is fair to say that governments have not responded. Is it because powerful political parties are funded in part by extremely wealthy interests? Over 40% of the delegates to recent climate change gatherings were lobbyists for fossil fuel interests. Could similar exertions of power apply to anti-wealth tax interests?

It could be pointed out that we seem to be unable to collect much of the taxes specified by current legislation. Perhaps we should work on that rather than on introducing new taxes. I would favour doing both, with the level of wealth tax so low, at least initially, that concerted legal effort to circumvent collection would be uneconomic. Enough of a policy intervention.

What brings about the prevailing levels of inequality? Why is it higher at some times and in some places than in others? Thomas Piketty hazards a bit of theory in this direction. He drew attention to two magnitudes, r, the return on capital, and g, the long-term rate of growth of the economy. He characterised r, the rate of return on capital, which is synonymous with the return on wealth, as being 5%, and g, the long-term rate of growth of the economy, as being 1%. These are reasonable 'stylised facts', as they are referred to in economics jargon, where illustrative numbers will do for the sake of argument instead of actual measurements. Several reviewers of Piketty made much of r and g, both as a new and significant way of viewing the economy and as a possible account for inequality. They were mistaken on both counts.

I yield to no one in my regard for Piketty and in support of his concerns. But r and g are not particularly informative in thinking about the economy and are of no help in explaining or understanding levels of wealth inequality and their changes over time and place. At first glance they seem to be saying something significant. Average long-term growth of the economy is a fraction of the return on capital, one-fifth to take Piketty's numbers. This must be revealing. The wealthy are not only much richer but are improving their positions as time goes by. Shocking. This is an inherent feature of the capitalist system, or so it seems.

First glances can be misleading and even totally wrong. In fairness to Piketty, he suggests in his lengthy book that r and g do not inevitably lead to the results he observes. Some reviewers have been less circumspect. Let's think about this in a simplified model. There are two groups, the workers get their income from work and the capitalists get their income from the return on capital. I know that some workers hold some capital, and some capitalists do some work. Ignoring this complication makes the analysis more tractable without biasing or distorting the results. Much of the skill of economists, and in other disciplines, lies in finding reasonably safely applied simplifications.

So, the capitalists earn 5% on their stock of capital and the workers get their wage. Suppose growth was zero. Would inequality increase? The comparison of r and g tells us nothing. If g is positive, who, or in what proportion, are the workers and the capitalists benefitting from growth? Again, r and g tell us nothing. How much of the growth is adding to the capital stock? What effect does this have on the return to capital and how does it affect wages? What about depreciation of the capital stock? And what about technical change? New ways of doing things and new inventions are big and complex issues. Is labour becoming more productive or is technical change reducing or enhancing the demand for labour? Comparing r and g reveals nothing about changes in inequality.

So much for the Piketty theory of inequality. Looking at the data, he notes a tendency for inequality to rise in normal, or business as usual, times, and to decline during upheaval such as a major war. Not surprising. Bombs can destroy some of the physical assets that shares and bonds lay claim to. And disrupting the economy can disturb wealth accumulating activity. But can we do better? Are there underlying trends towards inequality in a capitalist economy?

Just to clarify, we are talking here about essentially market economies. Russian oligarchs acquire riches through government promoted stealing of major industries. The Chinese path to inequality is similar in some respects with its own special wrinkles. I am directing attention to explanations of wealth inequality in market economies. It is surprising that this is a case of a missing theory. We just have no economic explanation of the levels and changes in this phenomenon. Economics can provide understanding of how varying degrees of monopoly power can generate higher returns to firms. This is a tiny part of the extreme wealth inequality story. That depends on the distribution of ownership of firms, monopolies, and others. There is some theory, more in the nature of observed behaviour, of how inequality changes over the course of economic development. But if we want a coherent economic theory of why inequality is less in Scandinavian countries than in the United

Kingdom, or why United States inequality is higher today than 50 years ago, we draw a blank.

It is generally agreed that there is a broad tendency in market economies towards increased wealth inequality. This broad tendency can be moderated, and even reversed, by some kinds of financial crises, natural disasters, wars, and most critically redistributive taxation. Taxation has the biggest and most lasting moderating effect. The underlying and persistent tendency towards increased wealth inequality is caused by intergenerational transfers.

In a competitive environment, some individuals do a bit better than others and some even a lot better. This is due to luck and other factors. This advantage is likely to cumulate over time and can be transferred to the next generation, typically through family members but not necessarily so. If there were no such transfers, with economic advantage passing from one cohort to the next, there would be no underlying tendency towards increased wealth inequality. The race would be re-run each period, with cumulative advantage halted. With the passing on of advantage, over time the greater relative advantage leads to ever greater advantage. Wealth transfer is the major factor, but educational and social advantages play a role.

Not all advantage is passed on successfully. Many chains of advantage come to an end from bad luck or folly. The advantage may be acquired by a new interest with no generational history. A few individuals become billionaires in one generation, and a few billionaires lose all their wealth. These events do not change the broad underlying tendency of economic advantage to cumulate and be passed on over time in one way or another.

Taxation is the main way in which the trend to wealth inequality can be halted. Direct transfers from the better-off to the less well-off can moderate the amount of intergenerational transfer of potential cumulative economic advantage. More important is the use of taxation to provide education, medical facilities, and a standard of living such that much of the population can take steps towards economic advantage.

Is this a common-sense description and broadly correct, and how might we test its accuracy? Maybe there is a very different and much better explanation of the level and changes in wealth inequality. My guess is that there is much room for refinement and detail in this explanation, but the crude simplistic picture it depicts has some validity. If so, that would account for why we have no economic theory of wealth inequality. So much of it depends on details of competition and transfers of wealth and advantage. The taxation element falls outside the domain of economics. Economics can tell us much about the consequences of different tax regimes, but little about when and why governments adopt one approach over another. For that we need historians, sociologists, and political scientists along with economists. This is a tall order, and a tight formal explanation must be a long way off. This topic was not included in the economics chapter because of its length and importance, but more because of it being a case of a missing theory. The fact that we lack a theory of wealth inequality does not mean that we cannot do anything about it. We could introduce a wealth tax.

7

Choosing an Adviser

Chapter 4 makes the case for choosing an economist as economic adviser. I hope it is persuasive. Anyone can claim to be an economist. There is no professional society that certifies competence. But the economic club, so to speak, has clear criteria of what it means to be an economist in terms of training and professional experience. The first steps in finding an adviser are not difficult. These are the standard procedures of collecting CVs and references.

The selection team can benefit from having an economist on board. But the final choice should not be left to him or her. Among the group of highly regarded and competent economists, some individuals would make good advisers, and some less so. Research achievements are the main drivers of reputations in economics. A good adviser will have some research experience, not necessarily at the highest level.

The research history of a potential adviser can be seen from his CV. A handful of publications in serious research journals is a sufficient indicator. Employment history is equally important. It is conceivable that a young recent graduate completing a Ph.D. might make a brilliant adviser, but the odds are heavily against this. The adviser needs to be an all-rounder. Some familiarity, if only passing familiarity, with many aspects of the economy is important. The adviser will have to deal with a great range of issues from how to fund medical services and education to national debt and monetary stability.

But that is not the compelling reason for a broad interest in the economy. A bigger consideration is the way in which economic policy moves are rarely tightly circumscribed in their effects. In a research study it may be appropriate to concentrate on core effects of economic relationships to discover particular relations. In policy matters slipover effects of a policy on other parts of the economy are important.

Research success in economics, as in other fields, typically comes from specialisation. A few researchers are just brilliant wherever they turn their attention in terms of techniques employed or in terms of subject matter. For many, specialisation leads to results. An ideal adviser is drawn to many aspects of the economy by sheer curiosity about what is going on.

Many economists have an employment history in academic work. University experience is a good thing. As Stephen Hawking once said, if I explain it to students enough, I finally understand it myself. Experience outside the university, or in addition to it, is important. Previous work as an economic adviser could be very revealing. Many jobs in economics have an element at least, of being an adviser. Some do not, such as economic journalism, a vital activity in a democracy. While some variety of employment is desirable, it is worth checking that employment was as an economist.

All this is standard in most searches for a suitable candidate. Now we can turn to the key considerations for an economic adviser. He must be an economist who is at home in considering the particular and the general, the abstract and the concrete, in the same flight of thought. This is the hallmark of the intellectually mature economist. How can the selectors detect these features?

A careful reading and absorption of the previous chapter is intended to go some way in arming the selectors with the necessary sensors. A few devices in preparing candidates prior to interview can be helpful. I strongly favour giving candidates time to prepare and advice in preparing is a good idea. Too often interviews discover who is a good interviewee, which may correlate weakly, if at all, with performing well.

Candidates could be asked to provide examples, real or made up, of models which failed to account for some facts. But could be improved by specifying relevant features of the context for applying the mode. Candidates could be asked to come prepared with examples of market failure and what might be done about them. They could be asked to discuss successful and unsuccessful privatising exercises and give some account for the different outcomes. Any discussion which made little or no reference to economic theory or which treated theory as sufficient in itself should raise warning signals.

Economies differ enormously in their natures and needs. A high-income country, a small country, a country with a specialised export profile. All are quite different. An adviser with an appreciation of the unique nature of the economy and its needs has an advantage. But no amount of local knowledge can substitute for knowing economics. Much of economic advice will have to do with fine-tuning in a business-as-usual setting. Occasionally an opportunity for a major change, or the unavoidable need for a major change, will present itself. Strength of character is an asset.

Throughout this discussion I have adopted the convention of writing about a single adviser. That is a device based on convenience. There may be several advisers, some based in the central bank, the treasury, regulatory bodies, and so on. A stand-alone advisory service may involve a team of advisers. This book does not address the issue of how economic advice should be deployed around government. That is for another day.

Time for a tale about advice that should have been given. Ghana was one of the first colonies to achieve independence. Economic development depended heavily on the export of cocoa. Timber and gold played a small part. There is no domestic demand for cocoa. A government body buys the entire crop. This is produced by many small farmers who plant and nurture their cocoa in an ecologically friendly way, mixed in with jungle growth. The crop is sold at world prices, and the farmers are paid about 10% of the current world price, and the balance is intended for development, including spending on an airline and three universities.

Rumour has it that sizeable amounts of cocoa are smuggled into the Ivory Coast, a short trek through the jungle at night. This is hard to police. People who know the area are likely to have close ties with the farmers and even be relatives. Strangers to the area would find it difficult to police the jungle routes to higher cocoa prices abroad.

The government is miffed at this smuggling which can be detected in what are taken to be national production figures. The government claims it is doing so much for the farmers, and yet some take cocoa to the Ivory Coast for higher prices. The government is right in its claim that it devotes resources to the farmers. This includes transport and marketing, research of cocoa disease and predators, road building, electricity and water supplies, roofing for houses, and sanitation.

A dramatic policy move might be to stop most of this help for the cocoa farmers, except possibly the disease and related research, a small factor in any case. Rather than support in kind, the farmers could be given money, perhaps even dollars along with local currency. If the money received by the farmers was less than the cost to the government of services in kind, the farmers might still be better off. This is a key aspect of the proposal. Is it reasonable?

There are several reasons why the farmers might be better off with more money but less than the cost of the government provided services. The farmers might prefer a different mix of provisions than that provided. They may be able to purchase services more competitively and efficiently than the official provision, over which they have no say. The option of deciding for themselves may be a benefit in its own right. And they also have the choice of not spending all the money and gradually building up a fund for future substantial investment, including investment in education.

Clearly the government would be better off under this arrangement, with more money available for development. In addition, the higher price for farmers' cocoa would reduce smuggling. The farmers win, and so does the government. Are there any losers? Quite possibly. The monopoly firms providing roads, water, and the rest may earn excessive profits. They may be powerful interests, appointed by the government and supportive of it. Some way of getting around this obstacle must be found to have the scheme adopted. If aid agencies approve of the scheme, they may have ways of effectively bribing the government to go for it.

The economic adviser needs more than scientific understanding of the workings of the economy. That may be nearly sufficient for some matters, such as issues of economic stability. Imagination and postulating alternative arrangements are of real importance. Will the cocoa farmers really be better off with more money and fewer government services?

Rarely will the adviser have the time and resources for an academic level study of this important question. The ability to improvise and approximate is essential. Along with this must go the ability to estimate the likelihood that any specific conclusion is correct. A popular jibe against economists is the request for a one-handed economist. Many politicians do not want to be told that on the one hand this and on the other hand that. Very funny. But does the politician really want to be told something is certain when it is uncertain? It sounds to me like the politician is asking the adviser to make the political decision and absolve the politician from political responsibility.

No doubt a good adviser needs diplomatic skills. A knowledge of the objectives and motives of the decision taker is useful for what is presented to government and how it is presented. This is one of the side issues along with others we have mentioned above. The central concern is knowledge of economics. Membership of the economics club is easy to determine. Degrees and a university appointment are part of CV information. References and employment in addition to academic employment can be revealing. The key issue is economic sophistication.

There are a few reasonably well-regarded economists, and even some highly regarded economists due to their publications, who believe broad elements of economic theory quite literally and are prepared to act on that belief. The outstanding example of this failing is an uncritical view of the market. Equally stupid, but less common among economists, is a negative view of the potential of the market. While this is uncommon, a short-run preference for efficiency is a more common liability.

Largely agricultural economies tend to give some protection to industry, and largely industrial economies tend to give protection to agriculture. These preferences can be exaggerated and misplaced, but they are not obviously foolish. In business-as-usual terms and efficiency considerations this protection is unjustified. That can be a mistake. People have preferences for kinds of work and for ways of life as well as for goods and services. An overly specialised economy may be weak in meeting these preferences.

Some degree of self-sufficiency may appear to go against efficiency concerns but provide a degree of insurance against international disruptions. Medical supplies and medical expertise fall into this category. Energy supply can take a long-term view with some efforts towards self-sufficiency. Food supply is another area for related considerations.

I have repeatedly used the term sophisticated as something to look for in an economic adviser. It is not a bad thing in almost any activity. I hope that the chapter on economics provides some guidance in choosing an economic adviser. My hope is that the government really wants an able adviser. Some politicians know what they want to do and want the adviser to be a rubber stamp. Of course, governments have a general idea of the kind of economy they favour. An adviser that can work with these objectives both sympathetically and critically is an asset.

The term capitalism covers a wide range of economies. What should be done by the market, along with how the market is regulated, is an aspect of this. It should be possible to entertain changes in the nature of the economy over time. Fundamental and repeated swings in direction are unhelpful. Repeated nationalising and privatising are likely to be destructive. Usually, in my view, the policymaker should aim to manage the economy better rather than to promote a different economy.

This is as far as I can go in choosing an economic adviser. My advice on choosing an adviser will improve the chances of making a good selection. We cannot do more than that. I wish selectors good luck. Several issues facing economies are important for the choice of adviser. These are discussed in the next chapter.

8

Prevailing Problems

Snippets on radio and television report changes in government borrowing or the exchange rate. A scripted authority, sometimes identified as an economist, repeats the statement of the presenter, presumably to lend some importance to the data. This information usually is the work of statisticians. In normal times, if there is such a thing, economists tinker with taxation suggestions or predictions about the exchange rate. Bigger issues that go to the heart of society have an economic aspect and could benefit from more concern by economists. Their potential contribution to understanding and to action is insufficiently recognised. They cannot be the day-to-day concern of the economic adviser. They boil away incessantly.

Who knows what lies in wait for us around the corner? Unpleasant and tragic surprises seem to be inevitable. The 'history is at an end' pronouncements are not just wrong, but tragically and ironically so. The idea was that liberal democracy would take hold everywhere. There would be an end to dictators and to wars. How hollow and grossly misleading that seems now.

Aggressive dictators are a problem for us all, both the citizens of those countries that are victim to them and the citizens of the liberal democratic countries. Should the West engage less with China and Russia? What is the economic cost to us of doing so? Received views have held that trading relations reduce the chances of military conflict. It also suggests that engagement, cultural, sporting, or whatever can soften hard dictatorships. Maybe. Economics is not very informative on that matter. Economics does come into it in estimating costs and potential policies regarding oligarchic inward investment and activity. The growing use of sanctions and asset freezing as tools of

© The Author(s), under exclusive license to Springer Nature Switzerland AG 2024
M. Steuer, *Dangerous Guesswork In Economic Policy*,
https://doi.org/10.1007/978-3-031-56078-1_8

persuasion have clear economic aspects and can benefit from improved understanding.

The drift to populism and worse in the remaining democracies is widespread. This suggests that some broad underlying factors are at work. Many pundits conjecture that social media has something to do with it. But no convincing causal explanations have been postulated. Very likely lots of factors are interacting in ways we do not understand, and maybe never will. Still, it is worth trying. My guess is that all the social sciences will have to contribute to an explanation if one is to be found.

Several more circumscribed problems will present challenges to most economies and to economic advisers. One of these is gross economic inequality. It is churlish to argue that unless you can specify the appropriate level or amount of inequality you cannot say there is too much. If the current levels are doing great harm, that is enough reason to start the programme of reducing inequality.

Oddly, in my view, some economists have maintained that inequality is not an issue for economists. They hold that inequality is a matter of values and is an issue for philosophy, not for a science with the objective of understanding what is going on. This is mistaken. Gross inequality has effects, and we can study those effects just as we can study anything else.

So, what are these effects? There are many, some relatively easy to see and some more elusive. Great inequality contributes to a general perception of and acceptance of unfairness. But is 1% of the population owning over half of the wealth unfair? Not a scientific question, you might say, wrongly. Most people have something approaching a common sense of fairness. If something violates that sense, that is a fact of life, like the speed of light. Whether this shared sense is meaningful, sensible, or appropriate is another matter.

Acquiring great stretches of Russia's natural resources for a pittance combined with mafia exertion is not earned income. American bungling of the privatisation of the Russian economy led to what was effectively violent acquisition of extreme wealth. Chinese billionaires benefitting from being in government tells a similar story. Inherited ownership of great stretches of valuable real estate is no better for having a longer history. Great wealth from leading giant corporations is not far off. Convincing evidence suggests that CEO talent is not in short supply and most individuals in such positions are not extraordinarily gifted.

Gross economic inequality distorts incentives. It favours short-term decision-making. It promotes efforts to secure certain positions rather than doing well in equally important other positions. The spending pattern of many individuals with extreme wealth has damaging consequences. Important areas of cities like London and New York are covered with unoccupied luxury dwellings. Property is a form of wealth holding like Picasso paintings, but with damaging consequences. What should be a thriving neighbourhood becomes a social desert. This development occupies space that could be used for residents to work and play and interact.

A good economic adviser will be sensitive to these harmful effects. He will be encouraged by a recent letter signed by 100 multimillionaires urging the introduction of a wealth tax. Some multimillionaires will migrate to avoid taxation. Several governments are pleased to receive them. Should we be concerned if those with extreme wealth choose to live and hold their wealth elsewhere? This is not a purely economic question, but it has important economic elements. Estimating the economic cost, if there is any, of driving Russian oligarchs and others of that ilk from the country is a potentially important contribution to the debate.

Taxation is central to any discussion of economic inequality. In my view too much attention goes to setting the various rates and too little to collecting the tax intended by legislation. A wealth tax for billionaires and other super rich has been mentioned. Part of the reason that gross inequality is accepted is the high level of wealth of those just below that level, and so on down the middle classes. Challenging the system may challenge the position of those who otherwise would see the injustice of extreme inequality. A review of trusts and individuals taxed as businesses is in order. So is a review of taxation based on the domicile of wives living in the various tax havens, rather than on where the income is earned.

Global warming is a societal problem tinged with schizophrenia. Year by year the evidence mounts, and the theory is both refined and supported. On one level most people, other than some anti-vaccination and wild conspiracy advocates, accept what the scientists say, namely, without drastic action now, and possibly even with it, catastrophe looms. Estimates differ. Some models suggest great horrors in 60 years and others say 80 years.

Economists tend to deduce what people believe from what they do rather than what they say, though there is some growing acceptance by economists of survey information. On the test of observed behaviour, people do not believe in the threat of global warming. Perhaps as the evidence mounts up this will change. Global warming is something of great concern to an economic adviser, whether asked for views by the government or not, because of his concern for the economy.

A permanent specialist body is needed to address the global warming issue. Countries vary enormously in how they are situated in the global warming crisis. Some island countries will disappear as the sea rises. Others will see flooding of key coastal cities. Populations will have to desert some countries as they become virtually unliveable, and others will be faced with billions of migrants. Much traditional food production will be impossible. Droughts, floods, and a general shortage of useful water will intensify. What does all this have to do with the economic adviser?

Efforts to reduce carbon emissions can be achieved through adopting new technologies as well as changes in consumption patterns. Some coal producers have made it clear that they will go on producing if the demand is there. Analogous to the cocaine story, consumer rejection of coal-based products may be more effective than trying to elicit promises from coal producers.

Economic policy can play a significant part in encouraging reduction in carbon emission with less disruption. It also can play a role in devising plans to deal with worst-case outcomes. Long-term planning for mass migration including internal relocation can be undertaken. Attempts at reducing the impact of worst-case projections is more than prudent. I see a permanent body doing this work, with constant interaction with the economic adviser, as the need for here and now action emerges.

The third horseman of the apocalypse is illustrated by the current pandemic. Planning and action for more plagues to come may yield great benefits at relatively little cost. The economics of lockdown needs serious investigation. Current knowledge does not go far beyond popular perceptions. Analysis of cross-country experience could be undertaken. An economic adviser needs some familiarity with these findings. At this stage the case for a degree of medical self-sufficiency appears strong. Policies to avoid a last-minute scramble for personal protective equipment would appear desirable, whatever virus or other disease comes forward.

Relentless population growth and ever more incursion into wildlife habitats strengthen the case for preparation. There are many ways of doing this, and economic advice could help in choosing between them.

Economic knowledge is a search for truth rather than an exercise in ideology. Several politicians seem to have no sense of truth telling or seeking, or perhaps they feel that short-run self-interest trumps the truth most of the time. They also appear to believe that the general public cannot detect lies or don't care about truth. Sadly, they may be more right than wrong in that belief. Much spreading of falsehood concerns economic matters.

I published a paper with colleagues about reports from head-hunter firms that many, if not most, CEO remunerations were too high. National press took up the story, as did radio and television, for a time. On the radio especially I was asked to debate with representatives of phony think tanks. They were paid to express a particular view and did so without regard for the truth.

Reasonable questions could have been raised about our findings, but that is another matter. The fact that mainstream outlets turned to these phonies is disturbing. A conspiracy? More likely intellectual and reporting laziness, as these ideology advocates are always ready to spout off.

It is disturbing to me that the economics club, to put it that way, does not feel any obligation to out these phonies who claim to be economists. Legitimate debate can go on about the appropriate role of government and what to regulate and how. To argue that a free hand for giant corporate polluters follows from something called economic knowledge is viciously wrong. Maybe there is little the economics club can do about it. Keeping quiet in the face of lies is tantamount to participating in them. Economic advice is relevant to the big societal issues like inequality, global warming, pandemics, reacting to aggressive dictatorships, and truthfulness in social debate.

9

Individual Virtues, Social Benefits

I start and end with the important notion that the economy is intimately interwoven with the whole social system. The economy is not just the market. It relates to all activity for making things and consuming things, whether done by a family, a government, or any other body. The economic aspect of interaction is not the only aspect. Gossip at the barbers is as important as haircutting. Whether and how people interact is influenced by the price of a haircut and many other things. The economy involves how we see ourselves, and how we relate to others. Can and should economic analysis and policy take some account of these considerations?

A group of economists have engaged in research and argument supporting the view that the goal of economic thinking and policy should be to promote happiness. To show that this well-meaning endeavour is mistaken requires an extended essay. In summary, happiness is an elusive objective. It is a welcome by-product of other things when it occurs. It can creep up on you unexpectedly, and it can elude you with no apparent reason. Short-run happiness can lead to long-run misery. Individuals vary, and perhaps it should be left to individuals as to how they balance happiness against competing objectives. The happiness goal can make policy unmanageably complicated. I am relieved that the happiness movement in economics is in decline.

The economic adviser will be aware of the intimacy and significance of economic matters to society generally, and how this relationship varies across countries and each society. In the previous chapter I discuss how economics considerations relate to major problems. In this chapter I emphasise the positive potential. There may be no harm in speculating whether and how policymakers may fruitfully give consideration to these possibilities. Maybe, just maybe, something useful will emerge from these unorthodox speculations.

Standard economic understanding sees work and production as a necessary evil in order to have consumption. Should we aim for the largest output from a given amount of work, or for the least amount of work for a given output? Neither. Profit maximisation in an ideal setting gives the appropriate solution. It achieves the right combination of the two tests of efficiency. This is an important insight from standard economics. The word ideal, meaning an appropriately competitive environment, is essential. Even so, the starting point of the analysis is flawed.

Satisfaction does not come from consumption alone. Indeed, some consumption can be better described as a tedious necessity. More to the point, work can be a vital source of satisfaction. No doubt the standard analysis of pain in work and pleasure in consumption is broadly correct for many people in rich countries and many more, proportionately, in poor countries. But it is far from universally applicable. I'll stick my neck out here. Educated people in better jobs, better by some standards, fail to see the satisfaction many gain in what the higher-up individuals perceive as less worthy. Regardless of how many people get nothing but pain from work, physical pain, boredom, anxiety, and alienation, many do not. Desirable and rewarding work is possible. An economy that promotes this is healthy and more successful, in my view, even with less output, and even with not quite the right mix of output.

Standard economic analysis judges success or the lack of it of an economy in terms of expanded choice for individuals. We add up all the benefits of everyone in the society. The higher that goes the better. Of course, we may take additional account of how these benefits are distributed across individuals. A few people getting the most benefit may not be a preferred outcome. But the starting point of this analysis is individual well-being. An entirely different and radical approach might be to ask how well the economy performs in promoting social values in the society.

Efficiency is important, and so is courage. We all have limited reserves of courage. And what we do have could be put to better purposes. A fear of economic insecurity drains courage. Survival can be the overriding concern. Taking a chance on a favoured career requires courage. Failure is a possibility. How costly that is depends in part on the welfare system. A society where courage is exercised is different from one where it is suppressed. The economy is not the only factor. Political repression can make huge demands on courage, demands that few can meet. But the economy plays a part in the exercise of the virtue of courage.

Time for a digression on the artificial intelligence and the end of work. In the 1930s especially a number of economists, including Keynes, looked to a period when enhanced mechanisation would take over a great deal of work. A universal payment system might be enacted to allow people to opt for a modest way of life without working. Those who chose to work could do so and receive income in addition to the universal payment. The growth of artificial intelligence has revived and enhanced this speculation.

There is some difficult economic analysis involved in making such a scheme operational. What minimal proportion of the population would have to work? What would be the differential income from working? And most important, who would own the capital that now produces so much with very little labour? Not much concrete analysis of these questions can be found in the current literature. Then there is the question of who should be entitled to income without work. Citizens of a certain age is a natural answer. And then there is the issue of keeping out other people who would be strongly drawn to the universal payment.

My view is that this is a long way off. Keynes and others had a vision of gentle folk with modest demands for goods and services and a strong preference for leisure activities, especially self-improvement along cultural lines. Enormous growth of income since the 1930s rather suggests otherwise. There seem to be no limits on the preference for a better car, a bigger house, a more elaborate holiday, including a brief journey into space. There appears to be a need for a large taxable economy to support education, health, and rescuing the disadvantaged, like the prison population.

No doubt artificial intelligence changes the mix and availability of so-called meaningful work, and perhaps work that gives job satisfaction. This is an issue for rich countries. Personally, I find the solution of importing cheaper labour from low-income countries unsatisfactory. Seasonal demands like fruit picking may be more acceptable. But the reliance on a permanent underclass fundamentally not part of the collective society goes against my sense of community. Is there scope for making much of work, including work displaced by artificial intelligence, more meaningful and more rewarding? Different work is a different thing from the little work economy. The market can do something, up to a point, but the bigger thrust must come from policy. Working from home makes some work more rewarding, but why did it take a pandemic to imitate this change? The answer is that some changes require coordinated action. The market typically guides individual action. This degradation highlights things the market is unlikely to do. There are others.

Curiosity goes hand in hand with courage. How does electricity work, and does this wage structure achieve its stated ends? Curiosity is the enemy of ideology. Some economic arrangements encourage understanding, or at least trying to understand. Some corporate cultures push the other way. Curiosity offers the best protection against the indoctrinator. Media is part of the economy. A high degree of uniformity and close linking of information to advertising stifles curiosity.

Social and economic policy on media and advertising can affect curiosity. Education has an even greater effect on curiosity. In most countries, if not all, education is partly in the market and partly provided through the public purse. In some African countries university education is free to the students who meet the entry standards. This is a considerable advantage to the better-off families who can more easily meet private schooling costs, and then get the benefits of free university education.

Better-off countries tend to support pre-university education from public funds, but charge students and their families for university education. The economic adviser must give attention to how the costs of education are met from the perspective of efficiency and ability to pay. It also impacts on the goals and objectives of education at different levels. Too much attention can be given to education as preparation for work.

Education is not the same thing as training to enable a person to perform a certain task. Results that are easier to measure may lead to rote learning. Promoting and encouraging curiosity may ultimately be better for training. It certainly is better for participating in society. What does this have to do with economics and the responsibilities of an economic adviser? Again, the economic perspective is part of the story, along with other parts. It can play its role including considerations of curiosity or take a narrower and more pragmatic viewpoint.

Courage and curiosity are linked to compassion. How far does compassion extend? I love all mankind. Really? The economy is a major factor in who we identify as close to us. No amount of effort or expense is too much for rescuing the little girl trapped in a well, or the sports team trapped by a flood in an underground cave. Maybe care for many occupying our prisons is more to the point. Who should get vaccinated, our neighbours or people in other countries? I do not expect economists to have the last word on such matters or even much to say. I do expect the economist to deplore arrangements which encourage concern only for oneself.

There are many potential hills to climb. One can aspire to being a scientist, an athlete, a musician, a worthy parent, a public servant, a poet, a skilled bus driver, a responsible farmer, a teacher, and on and on. A society that judges how high one has climbed up the chosen hill by the money earned is incapable of appreciating endeavour. A society in which money is the only hill is perverse. Economists have argued that the money hill is preferable to the political hill. A ranking according to power means that your climb higher lowers my position. Money is better. You can have more money without my having less money. Is that so? The amount of money I have may not change, but if money is the ranking metric, your advance lowers my ranking. Economists traditionally see more money solely in terms of affording more utility.

Utility is not like happiness or satisfaction. It is simply an ordering. With this much money I can go so high up my utility ordering. With more money I can go higher. How I order outcomes is up to me. Saving the snow leopards may be more important in my ordering than in yours. The relevant point is that money is usually thought of purely as a personal matter. Some thought has been given to conspicuous consumption: spending designed to impress others. In some capitalist societies money measures status. In others, less so. Some aspects of the economic system encourage concern for the individual and downgrade compassion.

For the decision-maker, there may be a preference between kinds of societies. For the economic adviser, there may be policy options that lean things one way or the other. Or it may be that too much concern with social status and too little appreciation of others falls outside the purview of economic policy. The economic adviser can do a lot, when advice is acted on, but there are limits.

10

The Adviser and the Government

The Adviser and the Government

It sounds like a romantic fairy tale. The truth is quite different. With luck, the government can secure an excellent economic adviser. There are no guarantees. With so many factors in addition to competence in economics needed for this job, selecting among possible candidates is not easy. A good grasp of the 'economics' chapter (Chap. 5) is the best preparation.

We ask a lot of the economic adviser. Central to the job is a broad, thorough, and sophisticated grasp of economic theory. The adviser has undergone years of training in mathematics that goes far beyond that of the other social sciences, and beyond that of most natural sciences. The adviser needs econometric skills. At the very least, ability at statistical inference must be strong enough to employ statistical investigation at a professional level.

Sophistication means knowing how to apply theories of how the economy works, what causes what, in an applied setting. The worst sin is to take it for granted that the market functions like the idealised market of general equilibrium theory. Holding to a faith that the *status quo,* as expressed in the workings of the market, as being both inevitable and desirable, marks out someone supporting special interests, not a competent adviser. The adviser will have a good understanding of market institutions and regulations that bring out better results from the market.

The economic adviser needs an insightful knowledge of the country and the economy he serves. This includes familiarity with a range of institutions such as commercial representatives, regulatory bodies, banking arrangements, trade unions, and so on. An advisory team is more realistic for covering such a range. But an economic adviser will be well placed to seek out the specialist skills and the information he needs.

No potential adviser will be a perfect candidate on all counts. Knowledge of economics is the only irreplaceable requirement. Will paying top dollar ensure securing the best adviser? Is this a perfect market, the more you pay the better the candidate? Unlikely. The most highly regarded economists are leading academic researchers and textbook writers. The adviser has related but different skills and less specialisation. A keen interest in the job is also essential. Paying more will not ensure the selectors find the best candidate.

Paying more may be a tactic for avoiding real responsibility. Alternatively, the selector should know as much as can reasonably be acquired about the task at hand. I paid top dollar may be a way of covering one's backside if a poor candidate is selected. A feel for what economics can contribute to policy is more likely to lead to a good choice.

Let's face it. The United States government does not need my instructions. Economic knowledge is firmly located in all relevant branches of government.

Whether it always prevails over short-run considerations, self-interest of the leaders, and ideological biases is another matter.

Dictators do not generally appear to need economic advice. They typically have a clear goal, large military expenditure, and a variety of offshore bank accounts. The economy pays the price. I set to one side the question of working for an unsavoury government. Clearly an adviser will not work for a truly wicked government. For appearances they can find a puppet adviser if they want one.

On the whole newer democracies are the target audience for this book. And here is the final digression. All new democracies seem to be prone to the same tragic mistake. The new democratic governments appear to want to be modern and to emulate older established democracies. Existing traditional institutions and power structures are swept aside. When Nkrumah took over in Ghana, he boasted that the chiefs would run away so fast they would leave their sandals behind. He was later deposed in a coup, and the chiefs are still there.

The case for an upper house reflecting traditional sources of authority, often themselves democratic in nature, is strong. Imposing a kind of Western style democracy on fragile governments is prone to failure. In Iran an upper chamber of Imams and other traditional leaders might have worked. I doubt if there had been an upper house of chiefs in Ghana there would have been coup after coup. If Afghanistan could have had an upper house with popularly supported war lords and sections of the Taliban, democracy might have held. The same argument could be made for Libya and many more fragile democracies that ignore traditional domestic structures. Critics can say I should stick to economics.

A suitable government and the right economic adviser have the potential to achieve a more prosperous society, and a more successful one in other regards. Hoping for miracles can detract from what can be achieved. Feasible steps to reduce the impact of impending tragedies are possible. Social developments that foster virtues have a chance of success. I think there are limits on the government providing a sense of achievement that can give meaning and pride to the populace. Most achievement and satisfaction are down to individual effort and good luck.

The mood of the current decades is likely to continue. This mood is very odd in some ways. Optimists tell us, rightly, that people are living longer, that the number of murders is declining, and all sorts of global measures show progress. And yet there is widespread unease and even pessimism. The general optimism of earlier decades has evaporated. Why? I tend to look at the economic factors while recognising that they are only a part of the story.

Extreme inequality has a major impact. We have the capacity to remove grinding poverty and do not do so. This is true of poverty even in the richest countries. Faith in the inevitability of progress is broadly seen to be misplaced. Our economic systems depend on thriving sectors producing new cars when the older models serve nearly as well. Clothing and many other expenditures fail to give promised enjoyment, but we need these sectors as tax bases to fund what does matter, health and education.

A possible way out would be to have more private expenditure on what matters. The challenge is to find a way of doing this while maintaining reasonable access to all. Large sections of the population get a bad start in life and never recover. Prisons are full of people we might try to rescue, but only minimal efforts are made. In large part all these issues come down to gross inequality.

A healthy society achieves some separation of wealth and power. The separation is never perfect but is sometimes kept within bounds. The present is not one of those times. Any serious change in tax collection for example is most unlikely. The power of media to shape public opinion is great. Subtle effects on education and the general perception of right and wrong are decisive. Just possibly a change could occur, but for now we cannot see how the existing power structure could allow that.

The *Readers Digest* publication had three core principles. The first was called eight to eighty, meaning it should cover all age groups. But people's interests change with age and vary in countless other ways. Do we really want to limit what we say to what everyone will understand and accept? Successful special arrangements and policy would be easier to achieve if we had more common or shared beliefs, attitudes, and preferences. The challenge of politics is to accommodate differences.

The second principle was called you could do it too. The idea was that if you were writing about a great scientific achievement like that of Einstein, or the skill and bravery of a skydiver who does a mid-air rescue of a colleague whose parachute failed to open, the article should suggest that you could do it too. No doubt people are capable of more than they think they can do, but the claim that there are no special skills and ability leads to populism and scorning the expert.

The third principle was we feel better. If you were writing about a war, a famine, or a natural disaster, you should give a spin to the story which was upbeat and optimistic. These three principles are the essence of populism. Keep the debate childishly simple. The instinct of the leader and his or her followers is all the knowledge needed. The words of the leader are intended to make the followers feel better, not to inform. Populism is the opposite of informed decision-making. A sub-theme of this book is that there is knowledge out there that can help. Part of this knowledge is in the economic sphere and part is in other areas. I am a betting man, and I fear that more irrationality will prevail, and things will get worse.

I have been encouraged to end on an upbeat note. Honesty forbids. I would like to at least end on an eloquent note, but ability prevents. What does encourage me is the James Webb telescope. This large device, covering the area of two tennis courts, had to be folded to fit into a rocket. Hundreds of complex mechanical steps were required to open it out. They all worked. And now the telescope sits out there in its chosen stationary orbit, millions of miles from the earth. Soon it will transmit images of the earliest stages of the universe back to earth. The motive for this great achievement may be tinged with regional competition. The basic motive is curiosity. We want to know. Perhaps a species that can do this will also avoid economic and political tragedy. The potential is there.

Whatever lies around the corner, clashes between democracy and dictatorship, natural disasters, population pressures, and self-inflicted harm from irresponsible policies, intuition and guesswork are not the answer. Highly trained expert advisers offer the best hope. All disciplines, biology, history, chemistry, English literature, geology, and linguistics, implicitly teach methods of thought along with their explicit contents. An appreciation of economics thinking is a hallmark of the concerned citizen and the informed voter. This is a path to better decision-makers who in turn have the ability to choose better economic advisers.

Acknowledgements

When asked which musicians had influenced him, the great jazz drummer Buddy Rich replied, all of them. Being open to many influences and not prey to a single-minded devotee to any school or individual is important. As a student at Columbia University, my Political Science Professor Fred Burin strongly encouraged my interest in social science and the possibility of my having something to say in this area. Progressive education at the Dalton School much earlier undoubtedly planted a seed. Lucky encounters with Jim Ball and Nancy Cartwright helped at two critical stages.

My biggest debt is to the staff and students at the London School of Economics. I must single out Dick Lipsey. He is a model of the devoted, imaginative, and thoughtful economist. Peter Abell and David Webb are also invaluable colleagues. Visiting the Economics Department at the University of Pennsylvania, then the Department of Ned Phelps, Karl Shell and Bob Summers, was a joy. Vodka martinis at the Departmental lunches on Fridays went down well.

I am grateful for my 3 years as Chairman of the Economics Department at the University of Ghana. The students were deeply engaged, and the staff were committed to advancing economic understanding. Working with Alex Kwapong, the Vice Chancellor, was a lesson in leadership and diplomacy.

More recently I have learned a lot from the students and the staff on the LSE Master's Degree in Economics and Philosophy. Afsa Aniffer comes to mind as one among many students who have affected my work. Weekly meetings with the LSE Behaviour Group led by Tom Dickins and including Andy

Wells, Richard Webb, Ben Dickins, Paul Taylor, and Edgar Porcher have given me a chance to try out several of the ideas in this book, as well as refining my understanding of scientific method.

Several lay persons, lay persons from the point of view of economics, read early drafts of this book and pointed out obscure and flagging sections. This was very helpful. They were Ellen Goldstein, Lynn Steuer, Dan Paton, Emma Oxley, and Caroline Murrell. Most encouraging, with one exception, they greatly enjoyed reading the book and felt they had learned something important. I won't say who the exception was.

Nick Stern and Alexa von Hirshberg have been extremely kind in helping to find a place for this book. Alan Budd has done the same. In addition, we had many discussions along the lines of the book.

My wife Christine is an impeccable proof-reader if that is the right word. More to the point, she has a nose for faltering argument and an eye for the flow and rhythm of written and spoken language. There are limits on what can be done, and bumpy passages remain.

Some readers of acknowledgements rightly expect to be acknowledged and are miffed at inadvertently being overlooked. Apologies.

Printed and bound by CPI Group (UK) Ltd, Croydon, CR0 4YY

09/10/2024

01042741-0004